New Beginnings

KARIN BRANDI

New Beginnings

For information:
Karin Brandi
PO Box 574
Cerrillos, NM 87010
karinbrandianimalart@gmail.com
www.karinbrandi.com
E-Book Available

Cover Art by Karin Brandi

Book Design by Barbara Fail

ISBN 978-0-692-96281-7
Karin Brandi
New Beginnings

The Now

The past has gone so very fast
It wasn't here at all it seems.
Who scooped it up? Where did it go?
Was it truly worth the effort we all know.
Or was it in our dreams?
Was it an illusion...as the New Agers say...
Is that what we are experiencing the rest of the day?
Or was it in our dreams?
Maybe that's all it is...illusionary stuff
It's only a life class of learning
A lifetime of yearning...
To be where we're supposed to be.
But not quite sure where that's at.
So...let's just go with the flow, as they say
Enjoy the rest of today.
If you know how, laugh, cry, smile, sigh...
That's all there is...The Now

By Juanita Somers Williams
(My Mother)

Introduction

A south wind is blowing this day in April, and the dust devils swirl round and round and sweep across the high desert landscape. White puffs of clouds drift slowly across the mesa as the ravens do their dance of flight within the bright blue, northern New Mexico sky. And as I remember why this book was written, the writing begins again.

Many questions have been asked of me...an ordinary woman who has had some extraordinary experiences. The most frequently asked question is why did you create an animal sanctuary? How did you become an artist? Why have you had numerous other-worldly and metaphysical experiences? And as the writing evolved I began to ask myself...why am I here? What is the purpose of life? And more importantly to me...what is my purpose?

As the exploration of my life began, I could see how sequences of events seemed to be perfectly orchestrated...one moment after another, and I believed writing of these experiences may benefit others. Then I remembered the promise...my promise to God...the promise which was made before entering this plane of existence. It was to write a book about my life. And so it began.

Through this book I share my life with you. I share my hopes and dreams with you. If you choose to take this journey with me, I truly hope it will assist you in some way, for my life has taken many twists and turns, many ups and downs, and many New Beginnings.

Within my writing I describe the expansion of my spiritual growth and how it occurred, my extraterrestrial encounters and metaphysical happenings, of which there were many. I relay the birth of my children, glimpses into the lives of my family, my friends, my three marriages, and my love of animals and artistic endeavors. For to me it is important to explain the choices made and to see the wisdom gained through each experience. Is this not why we are here...to express ourselves as best we can within a human form?

So you see, I have many reasons and a few credentials for writing this book, but most important to me, was my communication with God and my life experience...and what a life I have experienced. God is waiting to hear from all of you too.

May peace be with you always, love and abundance too.

Blessings to you my friend,

Karin

Chapter One

Prepare for another awakening soon. The tides will change as
the Great Mother shifts higher and higher in vibration.
And forms will expand as well to reach higher and higher,
and love will attain a new level and reign within
My Domain forever. There are no endings...only new beginnings.
There are no limits...simply a matter of choice. Stagnation or motion.
Movement is constant. Change is fulfilling and adaptability is the key.
Your heart knows no boundaries and the infinite is reachable within
the divine guidance of love perpetuated through the heart.
As the earth sheds her skin, so do her inhabitants, and that
which is "within" will be revealed.
As the true reality begins to implode on those who partake of her body,
all will regain their sovereignty and learn to breathe and
become a light unto their own self. It is time.
Share your gifts, my daughter. Speak your truth.

ZANESVILLE, OHIO – 1961

Lying very still within the tall and so very green grass of southeastern Ohio, rolling hills surround me and white puffs of clouds drift over my head and cover the skies...and the sun speaks to me, showers me with smiles and promises of new beginnings. A curious filly sniffs my breath and I shake inside knowing my friends are watching. Her mother senses fear and comes to her baby immediately. She looks down at me, fascinated for a moment, and allows me to gently place a handmade lead rope over her body and slowly I climb upon her back. Oh no. She remembers "this" and gallops as fast as she is able to release me, the intruder of her peace. I laugh hysterically as she comes dangerously close to barbed wire fences in her attempt to wipe me, this terrible creature, off her body. Ducking as she runs under low-hanging branches of trees, I finally fall off as her next attempt is in plain sight... the barn door, where she would have injured or severely scraped my leg. I am eight years old and fearless...at least with animals. My friends are running to me...alive and nothing broken, we walk towards water and drink as it flows through our fingers into an unpolluted stream.

CERRILLOS, NEW MEXICO – MARCH 2012
OLD WINDMILL TRAIL

I have returned from Madrid, a nearby village, once an old coal mining town, now filled with colorful characters and artists and galleries and tourists from all over the world. Over a diet coke with a customer at the Mine Shaft Tavern who was making a final payment on a horse painting, a suggestion was made, or almost insisted upon, that a book should be written by me...and so it begins. At times I have a tendency to talk too much...about animals that is. Yet she was right. There is much to say.

My neighbor, Judy, calls as I check on my 41-year-old gelding through a horse-licked window and concentrate on her voice...he is fine. She congratulates me. Your new horse mural will be beautiful, she says. The March winds are singing so loudly they distract my focus with only 35 minutes before I begin...feeding will be difficult. The horses are calm, yet waiting, and the cows have not arrived. Thirty minutes to go. The skies are pale as the dust flies and dulls the bright blue skies and dims the mountains. A storm approaches. It is time to feed.

What has happened, I ask, awakening at 5:01 AM the next morning to a bedroom filled with light. Looking outside, a full moon is illuminating the high desert landscape which is covered with three inches of new snow. How magnificent, how beautiful it is, and a great sadness comes over me. Will this be the last time I see snow?

It is 6:30 AM and he is cold and hungry and my elderly horse Snowy whinnies loudly for food. Always the gentleman, he allows me to enter his domain with his meal, consisting of senior equine sprinkled with barley and hot water, a side of chopped carrots, and finely shredded hay. My favorite time of the day is the first moments spent with him. His power and calmness and the sound of his gentle chewing surround me and give me strength as I stroke his neck. How blessed am I?

A raven named Rachael lands on a fence post waiting for her meal as the coyotes dart back and forth making snow tracks on the sacred hill, hungry and waiting. Rachael acknowledges my voice by looking up and down and being flattered and fluffing up her feathers, before she lands on a meal of cracked corn and table scraps. Her job is quite important as she calls her friends to breakfast. Four coyotes zigzag their way down the hill to their meal of dry dog food. Diego and Big Daddy are present. It is so good to see my old friends as they have been around for such a long time...almost the beginning. And they understand the rules, such honorable coyotes they are...never attacking any of the animals.

CERRILLOS, NEW MEXICO – FEBRUARY 2002
OLD WINDMILL TRAIL

It was a long, long drive, and he drove so slowly over the rocks and treacherous turns and hills and axle-breaking bumps in his huge white double-cab pick-up, with me sitting in the passenger seat. You must know how much worse a bumpy road can be, riding on the passenger side of a pick-up. And the nausea set in. Six miles took us through many of his colorful jokes and over 30 minutes of time, so careful he was until we reached the destination...our newly purchased property. Bryan said, "where?" in his Texan accent. "Up there," I said, pointing to the hill I fell in love with. "Just kiddin' ya. Already knew where it was," he said, walking straight to the spot. Not surprising to me as I knew him well in this life and very well in past ones in which we both felt we had been more than just friends. "Didn't have to dowse it, already knew you had Indian spirits here," he said. There were two junipers on the small hill which was covered with an assortment of white rocks and at the very top and centered perfectly between the junipers were two large stones. "Put your feet right here," he said, "one foot on each rock and feel the energy and look."

"Now what do ya see? You can see all of the mountain ranges in the area...the Ortiz, over there, the Jemez, the huge Sandia, there's Big Baldy above Santa Fe, and the Cerrillos Hills." At that moment tears began to appear in both of our eyes as we stood silent for a moment until he spoke. "Your father attempted to heal your body here on the spot of the two rocks, on this sacred hill long ago. You were a member of the Anasazi and your father was the medicine man of the tribe. You took ill and he brought ya here for healing. He is here right now, over there by the juniper." For a second I saw him and the tears increased and then the image was gone. "You cannot build your house on this hill. It is sacred ground, ya know. It would disturb the spirits. May be a burial site, not really sure, but it was used to communicate with others...probably with smoke signals, since you can see all the other mountains," he said. "OK," I said, looking up at the tall Texan, long and lean, wearing a tan cowboy hat, sunglasses, my friend and neighbor from Goldmine Road...a kindred spirit of sorts. "We won't."

"Also, you're gonna paint again, Karin," he said with certainty. "Oh no I won't." "I'm tellin ya, you will," he said. Starting to shake my head, he ignored me and said "I see all sorts of animals...horses... maybe an Indian or two, spirits. You will." Two years later I sent him a matted print of one of my many horse paintings and at some point I painted a Native American...an Anasazi whose name was Running Elk. He was a white buffalo warrior who was the medicine man of a tribe and my father who attempted healing me upon the sacred hill many lifetimes ago, after being injured by a mountain lion. His portrait hangs in my bedroom and his spirit watches over me at night.

Yes, Bryan was and still is a teacher to me. He is 20 some years older and the best dowser in New Mexico, written about in many books. He could charm the rattles from a rattlesnake. Gruff in speech, he pulls no punches and gets straight to the point, and the heart. He has a joke for every occasion, but also taught me a very valuable lesson. It is to never offer advice unless you are asked, even if you know what they are doing will not work for them or cause them pain. "It'll just piss em off," he said.

CERRILLOS, NEW MEXICO – OCTOBER 2001
OLD WINDMILL TRAIL

Andy and I are constructing our new home on 42 acres. The foundation site in front of the sacred hill (at Bryan's suggestion.) The land is nestled within a valley surrounded by mountains and covered with the northern New Mexican skies. The peace and calmness of the land speaks to me of its healing properties...but this is like the wild west and oh my God what WAS I thinking? And why did I agree to do this? My frame is small and the work never ending and I am almost 50 years and at times wine is my pain killer and trusted friend. An empathic person like myself can feel the cry of every plant and rock, so all must be removed and replanted from the foundation before the building can begin. There is no electric power, no phone lines, no gas or water except for a well, so a solar system has been installed. Many hours of back-breaking work have begun and a divorce occurs because of it as I do not take orders well...and yet a phoenix arises to take its place.

Another beginning for others...those of four legs.

One late afternoon as we are working on the house foundation a wild bull saunters down his familiar path heading for the pond, for water, and has to make a detour around the new fencing for the chicken coop. A windmill and stock tanks were already in place which gave us the only water available for animals in the entire valley. The bull is enormous and dark and snorting and dust flies as he scrapes the ground with his hooves. His anger is felt strongly by both of us and I gently walk towards him speaking in soft tones. Andy is standing with our dog, Nikky, who is barking loudly as Andy prepares for battle...a rake his only weapon. An energy takes over my body and my heart connects with the bull. Over and over I silently tell him how much he is loved, how beautiful he is...and he can hear me and stares at me and quiets for a few moments until he remembers what is happening. This is MY land, not your land he says to me. Go away, he tells me! And the quiet voice begins inside of me again, only this time it tells him, "be aware of the battle which will ensue and that he may win but become terribly injured," and a vision appears showing him his injuries from the rake. The giant bull hesitates, then slowly walks away. Andy and I collapse to the ground. "What on earth were you thinking," he yells at me. Yet he was not frightened for himself. It was for me.

ZANESVILLE, OHIO – OCTOBER 1996

My children, Ryan and Somer, and I returned to my hometown of Zanesville, Ohio seven years ago following my divorce from their father in Clearwater, Florida...my second divorce. It has been a long and arduous journey becoming a single parent and especially difficult for my children. But much assistance was given to me from my family, my brother and sister-in-law and especially my parents, with whom we lived for over nine months. I now have a fantastic job as the art director of an embroidery company, and recently purchased a small but comfortable house within an old but well-established neighborhood near the elementary school my children attend. The street is lined with tall maple and elm trees, and Halloween decorations and fall flowers of red and pink and gold are visible on every porch. The smell of fall is in the air...my favorite time of the year. How much better can it get, I contemplated while sitting outside one warm October afternoon sipping a beer. You must know that when the Universe is challenged, (and I so dislike the word "challenge",) it answers you, and not necessarily in the way you might think.

A week later I walked into a gym to retrieve my daughter and her friend after their gymnastics class and almost stumbled over a tall, dark-looking man sitting on the floor. He asks, "which one is she? " "The pretty one with the blonde hair," was my curt reply. "She should be taking ballet classes," he said with authority. "She is the best one in this class," I said, while thinking she is the best one at anything she sets her mind to do. Years later he would prove to be correct, however at that moment warning flags were felt like tiny pricks all over my entire body. Yet he was intriguing with dark eyes that had felt much pain...they were familiar. Perhaps a soul mate? And we talked. His name was Andy and he was waiting for his karate class to begin and he was a teacher at an elementary school where two of my friends taught. Coincidence? There are none. "My phone number is in the book," not wishing to waste any more of my precious single parent time on him..."or you could ask one of my friends."

He called two days later as my friend Vicki, a teacher at the school, gave him my number...and he called every night for a week, and his voice could melt the snow on a cold winter's morning and his insight was astounding. We had our first official meeting over wine and chicken and candlelight and roses at his favorite hometown restaurant Adornetto's. It was Veteran's Day...a significant day for him as he had fought in the Viet Nam War where most of his soul still resided. Although I did not know this yet. And my heart pleaded and begged and won over all logic and within nine months we were married at the Little White Chapel in Las Vegas and my heart sang. And I loved him, oh how I loved him.

Just an aside. When you ask for a soul mate, it does not mean the heavens open up and twinkling stars appear and sweet white doves are flying all around you. That person came to TEACH YOU because you asked to be taught. The lesson is not always an easy one. But you probably already knew. It took me a long, long time to learn this.

Chapter Two

The book will come more swiftly as you quiet the brain and listen,
and become aware as it flows into your conscious self
to be written in coherent form...
always as the observer and through the heart.

ZANESVILLE, OHIO – 1958

"Mommy, why does it smell so bad? Where are they taking them?" Sunday afternoons were sometimes spent taking a drive out into the country with my parents. My mother loved to look at houses and flowers, and search for bittersweet when in season, and my father loved my mother. My brother, Ken, and I ate ice cream cones from the Dairy Queen and fought each other in the back seat while our little dog, Carmel, sitting on my mother's lap, barked out the window at anything that moved. A huge truck filled with cows passed by on one of the drives, and the smell, and their moans and groans, hurt my five-year-old heart to its deepest core. "Where are they going? Hamburgers come from cows?"

ZANESVILLE, OHIO – 1995

She was so pretty I disliked her immediately and she was also hired against my protests. Yet messengers come in many forms and she admired me and wished to become my friend. Oh dear God, how can this be? A tall slim dancer/artist entered my life...one who will not be forgotten. I was working at my job as the art director at the embroidery company, and she worked for me.

Oh, now what, I thought as she entered my office one Monday morning. Accidents followed her wherever she went. Perhaps another one? She looked at a photograph taken less than six months ago and asked, "when were you married? You looked so young!" "Less than a year ago," was my reply. Reading her thoughts I could see her thinking, well how could you possibly have aged so quickly? Honest and innocent, she spoke the truth...rare, I thought, very rare. My attempt to escape with an excuse did not work and she began to tell me her story and what happened the first day she moved in with her soon-to-be husband. He came from a powerful family who owned the largest slaughterhouse in town, and the slaughterhouse was located next to her new home. "Yesterday, cows were brought in from several trucks," she said..."and it was awful...there were so many..." The noise from the mooing and moans as they prodded them with sticks and kicked and shoved them down the well-worn path to the barn had made her physically ill. The gunshots were heard for hours. "Certainly they did not know what was about to happen," I said. "Oh they knew," she said. "They knew."

CERRILLOS, NEW MEXICO – 2001
OLD WINDMILL TRAIL

The house was a work in progress...an ongoing backbreaking kind of progress. We were living in a small trailer purchased from a man named Ken for $500.00 who lived at the front of the old dirt road. He helped us move our sixteen chickens from our previous residence several weeks ago and they were adjusting to their new coop and living quarters. Our home on Goldmine Road was sold and no longer were we traveling back and forth to work on the house. Our tiny trailer was barely sufficient, but held our bed, a table and chairs, and had a stove, small refrigerator, toilet, bath tub and shower of sorts. The pipes would freeze no matter how many straw bales were placed around them and water had to be hauled by buckets from the cistern near the house. Eventually the toilet froze up as well. Nikky and our cat, Annie, slept with us and gave us warmth as the cold November winds began to howl. The endless pounding of nails and exterior painting continued. Some friends, Ann and Greg, and Marilyn and JB came to help on weekends. It was such fun to see them. "You look so tired, Karin," Ann said. "God, girl, you need some rest," observed Greg.

But as you all know magic can appear in even the darkest of experiences. And it did. Andy was working at the windmill one day and came back to the house breathless and smiling. I had not seen a smile on his face for such a long time. "I saw the most beautiful grey horse running through the pond just now. Do you think there are wild horses out here too?"

And several days later they came...and our lives would be forever changed. Three beautiful mares and an old white gelding appeared and it was magical! The teachers had arrived and we gave them apples and we named them. The small white gelding was named Snow and we learned later that this had been his name for many years. The tall grey mare with the most beautiful dark brown eyes that sparkled with light was named Ci-Ci. She was part appaloosa and part goddess with a broomstick tail, and every male who came within her presence was mesmerized...and that means equine or human. The tall powerful buckskin was named Star. She had strips of white fur around her legs from old injuries. Strong and mean but kind-hearted, she led the cast of four. The tiny brown mare was named Co-Co. Later we learned she was a wild mustang captured not far from here in Cedar Crest. Her eyes were dark and her spirit captivating.

A promise was made that day as we could feel their anguish at being reduced to begging. It was only November, not yet winter, but there was little or no graze, and Snow looked very ill and all were quite thin. "We will make it better for you." And Star could hear our thoughts and said they would return. Andy purchased some hay from the local feed store the next day and they returned as promised and the teachers began to teach the students. And we listened and learned. The healing began and so did our promise.

We asked everyone we knew who they belonged to and they explained that "wild horses just live out here," or "that white one has been around for ten years or so." One day I asked the right person and she told me the horses had belonged to her husband who released them to the valley when they could no longer be ridden many years ago, giving them their freedom. In his manner of thought, it was the honorable thing to do as none of them were able to be ridden. Snow was too old, Ci-Ci could never be saddle-broken, Star had been caught in barbed wire and severely cut, and Co-Co had hoof problems.

We gradually came to the realization that we now "owned" the four horses and with little or no experience began the learning process of caring for them along with the construction of our new home. There was a definite learning curve involved, as my experience with horses was limited to riding the Shetland ponies as a child and with friends upon occasion. Andy had a brief job experience of training camels at the San Francisco Zoo. Never in my wildest dreams would I ever have even considered the possibility of this occurring. Never. And yet looking back through my entire life I could see where all experiences led to this point. My children were now living their own lives, no longer needing me in quite the same way and the horses helped to fill the empty space in my heart. And there was purpose and meaning to my life.

Within a few weeks a young grey appaloosa gelding galloped into our lives and straight into my heart. And what a disturber of the peace he was...challenging Snow, starting fights, and simply harassing all of them. He was wearing a halter but we knew no one in the valley at that time to call, so he stayed until one day the owner showed up on horseback. His name was George. He was short, Hispanic, cruel to his horse, and spoke little English. I disliked him immediately. In half English, half Spanish he told us the Blue Corn Appaloosa was recently purchased from the Santo Domingo Pueblo.

George brought him home and the horse escaped while being tied to a stake without food or water for three days in an effort to saddle break him. You cannot imagine what I was thinking upon hearing this but had to contain myself. Also, I do believe there are some horses who are not meant to be ridden...simply my opinion. He started towards the gelding, rope in hand, but Star trotted between them, blocking his attempts. I yelled, "I would watch out for her if I were you" and he retreated a bit, circling around to get to his horse and out of Star's way. She could be intimidating when need be, and this was a good time. Andy whispered to me, "why don't we buy him. We have the money, let's do it." While shaking my head yes, he called George back and we bought the horse. I named him Stallone. It took quite awhile for Stallone to forget his horrible experience and to allow us near him, however he became the comedian of the group...learning to turn on outside water faucets and delight in the running water. He was adept at unlocking gates. To this day all gate locks must be Stallone tested before they are used.

It was during this time that I saw something in this world, from another world. Please have an open mind as you read this. It is the truth as I see it. We were building our house in such an isolated area, that many of the wild animals and birds we encountered had not ever seen human beings. Some simply did not like us being here...at first. One morning while washing my dishes, I heard Nikky barking fiercely. I ran outside to see why he was barking , and there before my third dimensional eyes were two very strange looking animals. At first they looked like sheep, but as I came closer to them I could see they were not.

They had canine features and were covered in white sheep-like fur with a golden tinge. One was rather large...perhaps sixty or seventy pounds. The other, much smaller. Their short tails were wagging and their faces smiling as they watched Nikky with delight. I called them "sheep-dogs." As soon as they saw me, they ran off so quickly they seemed to disappear. Several weeks later, I spotted them again while walking down our driveway to the pond. They were drinking water from the stock tanks, and although I was walking as silently as possible, they turned, saw me and began to run away. But this is the strange part. I was on higher ground than them and watched them run, faster than any creature on Earth. Within approximately five seconds they were out of my sight, and I could see for miles around me. How could they possibly belong to this planet?

I asked at a private channeling session with a woman in Albuquerque, several months later, who the strange animals were and was simply informed they were placed here by beings from another planet. They were told not to interact with human beings because human beings were dangerous.

The winds of the valley began to blow with ferocity and whispered the promise of winter and the sky sputtered light flurries of snow onto the high desert. We began to spot cattle in the distance, roaming and eating cactus, of all things. They came closer, attracted to the hay we were feeding the horses. I began to carry hay out to them, sometimes chasing them in the fields as they appeared so thin to my Ohio born eyes. And they came closer and closer until one day they stayed. The enormous bull, black and white in color with a rack of horns five feet wide, I named Calvin. He touched my heart and coming close to him without fear, well it just made my day. It did. With him were four females. One, his "girlfriend" of sorts, with horns to match his own, we named Dominique. Scarlet was the name chosen for the oldest and wisest cow, and her calf was named Rosie. The large cow with chunks of skin missing from her ears due to the wild dogs in the area, came to be known as Momacita. She was obviously pregnant. The month of January brought us two more...Claire and her calf Gabriel. Gabriel grew into an enormous steer, greatly respected by the rest of the herd and greatly loved by us. Anyone who decided to make the long journey to our land met Gabriel and fed him carrots. He expected and received no less.

Chapter Three

Love well. Love deeply.
For there is no greater force
within this segment of Creation.

COLUMBUS, OHIO – 1982

It was another cold March day, the kind that are typical in Ohio at that time of year, with overcast skies. My friend, Lois, and I were having dinner at our favorite restaurant Houlihans, on her twenty-seventh birthday. We both worked 9 to 5 jobs but also were belly dancers upon occasion, making extra money and performing at various functions. Music could be heard playing softly in the back-ground and it was a peaceful and quiet evening, exactly as we had planned until...a tall blonde-haired and very attractive man attempted eye contact with me. I was with my girlfriend and "not interested," I said when he asked me to dance. "She is opening presents, maybe later." His blue eyes are bright and piercing and there is a small scar under his left eye. He returned and Lois said to me in a low whisper, "if you don't dance with him, I will." One dance. Just one dance was all it took and the father of my children entered my life. His name was Larry and although unknown to me at the time, I was balancing a Karmic debt with him. And what a rollercoaster ride my life was about to become.

COLUMBUS, OHIO – SEPTEMBER 2, 1983

No one told me it would be like this!!!! No One!!! Thirty-six hours I have been in labor and many more hours to go, they told me. The wash cloth Larry has been using to wipe my brow is thrown at him and misses. My aim was bad but it did hit the attending physician and quietly the interns were asked to leave. There will be no more men watching my progress, but the painful monitor remains in place. When will my son make his entrance? My requests for a painkiller were denied since I signed the paperwork for a drug-free birth. The screaming became low guttural moans as the pain took over my body and in a low voice I whispered, "please God. Please help me."

My mind drifted to several years past when "once upon a time" two gynecologists from the same practice informed me that it would be virtually impossible to become pregnant. "You could do some sort of fertilization," one of them suggested. But this was no fairytale it was MY life. Apparently my body and soul had other ideas and wanted a child and after all doctors are merely "practicing" medicine, or so I've been told.

Most of my pregnancy was spent alone. I had been working for several years as the Assistant Art Director at a large silkscreen company called Roach, Inc., in Columbus, Ohio, and aside from belly dancing, my job was my life...my entire life. I was the only woman to not only survive the all male art department, but also become the Assistant Art Director. Within a year of my first meeting with Larry, and with great astonishment, I became pregnant. Larry and I were married by a judge in a Columbus, Ohio courtroom when I was four months "along" and he left for a new job in Rochester, New York the next day. As you might suspect he and I considered the marriage for quite a while. Well it was more him than me as I feared the prospect of becoming a single mother and wished for my baby to have a father. It was a horribly emotional time for me and I stayed in Ohio as my company had great insurance and would pay for the birth of my baby. And now he is coming.

This morning I drove to the office of my OB-GYN at the suggestion of a friend and went home to call my mother and my husband to tell them that my son would be arriving soon. My mother spent the day with me trying to make me laugh as we sat outside watching squirrels fighting each other while gathering nuts until Larry arrived, just in time to drive me to the hospital. (Or so I thought.) And here I am and it has been hours of agony until an angel in white appeared with a bit of Demerol for me. She said, "you need this to sleep a few seconds between contractions." "Thank you, God," I whispered. And finally my gentle peacemaker, my son, Ryan, made his entrance into this plane of duality. My heart filled with love and awe of this tiny being who had been residing within my body for so long. As they whisked him away for tests I missed him after being within his presence for but a moment. He is an "Indigo Child," filled with the love of spirit and faced with many tasks in his lifetime. My son. I must say that to this day, I enjoy every moment spent with him. He was born with extraordinary wisdom, for one as young as he, and changed me into a loving and caring woman. He taught me to love.

CERRILLOS, NEW MEXICO – SEPTEMBER 2011
OLD WINDMILL TRAIL

My cell phone sang its song early one morning and the clock read 5:30 AM something. Who would in their right mind be calling me this early? My body staggered to the phone. It was Larry, and unable to focus I decided to call him later after the morning chores. Listening to the message several hours later, he said, "thought you'd be up early," in his Ohio drawl and, "call me later when you can talk. Nothin' important." Later came and I called him but he was in the process of cutting down a tree. "Why? Why are you cutting down a tree, Larry?" I asked in my best tree-hugger voice.

"Just don't like it," he said with heavy breathing. "Can't talk now, catch you later, Hon," and I could hear the buzz saw starting in the background.

Five days later he called. "Karin, you'll never guess where I am. I'm in a daggone hospital," he told me. "Oh crap. What's going on, Larry?" I said with concern and worry. We had our "ups and downs" over the years, but I still cared for him. He contracted Hepatitis C during the Viet Nam War due to a physician using the same needle on an entire troop. All but a few men had already passed to the other side and Larry had been on a liver transplant list and in and out of hospitals for many years. He told me that in the process of cutting down his tree, a limb fell on top of him, and he passed out with several broken ribs. A neighbor saw him and called for an ambulance. "Well, Hon," he said low in his throat, "they found a tumor in my liver and it is inoperable." "I'll call the kids, Larry. It will be OK, Larry," I said while thinking how am I going to do this since he hasn't spoken to either one of them in years. "Yeh," he said, "but what am I gonna do about Tyler?"

CLEAR LAKE CITY, TEXAS – OCTOBER 1984

My introduction to Texas was a truck stop filled with men and women driving pick-ups, wearing cowboy boots and hats and speaking with a musical southern accent that I love hearing to this day. Hmmm, this might be fun, I thought as we left the truck stop and headed for Houston.

Larry was doing extraordinarily well with his new job and was promoted to Sales Director for all of Texas, and eventually became Director of the truck drivers training school he worked for as well. After living in a corporate apartment for several months we purchased a home on El Dorado Boulevard, a few blocks from NASA in Clear Lake City near the Gulf Freeway...a twenty minute drive to Galveston. We were practically surrounded by water and could go to the dock and buy fresh seafood daily when the fishermen unloaded their catch. Larry traveled more than expected, yet I was happy decorating my new home, caring for Ryan, the love of my life, and painting whenever I could.

CLEAR LAKE CITY, TEXAS – OCTOBER 1985

She came to me in a dream as a small child about the age of three. She was dancing in golden light with the most enormous grin upon her angelic face. She spoke of much, yet I retained none of that which she told me. Who was she...this child of light? I would soon find out.

My doctor confirmed it. I was about six weeks pregnant, but there was a complication. "You have what is known as cervical dysplasia... pre-cancerous cells on your cervix. We can do an abortion next week," he said. "I would not allow my wife to carry a baby to term with dysplasia as there is a slight risk," he said. "The birth may cause the cancer to form and spread." My heart was pounding and my mind racing and "absolutely not" was my first thought. I remembered the two gynecologists in Ohio who told me I could never become pregnant, yet here I was in the second month of my second pregnancy. "I will not have an abortion," was my reply. "Then you will have to take very good care of yourself...rest every day and eat well," he informed me. I had no doubt that I would be fine, but gave a two week notice at my job as a dance instructor at pre-schools that very next day. Larry was working and traveling and seldom home, but everything would work out perfectly. Within a few months "she" took control of my body...the little one in my dream. She would not tolerate meat of any kind even though my body became anemic and my weekly beer became a thing of the past as she would kick and squirm until I put it down. I loved her already.

CLEAR LAKE CITY, TEXAS – JUNE 26, 1986

The wind was howling and blowing, and pounding my house and my head. Blankets had been nailed against all windows and doors and extra food and water were purchased this morning. Larry arrived before the storm and was busy preparing the walk-in closet with Ryan, making it an adventure for him. The familiar pains began several hours ago but were so far apart I knew there was plenty of time. Larry and Ryan climbed into their sleeping bags and I climbed into bed with a feeling of something not being quite right. In less than an hour I woke Larry and told him it was time to go to the hospital. The contractions were increasing in severity and coming closer and closer together. We all got into the car and headed for the babysitter to drop off Ryan, dodging tree limbs that cluttered the streets, amid the horrible crashing of thunder and clashes of lightening. Hurricane Bonnie would make landfall that night somewhere near Galveston. The trip to the hospital took forever and as the pains became closer, my fear increased. My daughter is coming. She is coming.

Finally the hospital came into sight and Larry wheeled me through the door. There was not time to check in, so a nurse rushed me to an emergency room where she informed me that I must not, under any circumstances, have my baby until a doctor arrives. "You see," she said, "all of the doctors are attending a meeting in Houston and the Gulf Freeway is closed down due to the hurricane. There is only one doctor in this hospital that can deliver a baby and he is with another woman." "Well, this is my second pregnancy and I know she is coming any minute," I said through clenched teeth as my daughter began to make her dramatic arrival, and my body could not stop it from happening. I had to push. Within a few minutes she was with me...wrapped in a blanket, lying beside me, all pink and beautiful and wide eyed. "Oh my God. Why isn't she crying? What is wrong? Is something wrong with her?" The nurse replied, "this is what a healthy baby looks like. She is fine." I stared at her in awe and wonder and love...my precious little girl of the Golden Light. A Golden Child. The doctor arrived and took her from me and the stitches began. A few hours later my sister-in-law called and said to use the name Somer if I wished. (It was a name she had chosen for one of her children.) She said, she might not ever have a girl (which turned out to be true) and the baby was due on June 21st wasn't she? The name was meant for her. My mother's maiden name was Somers and it seemed to be the right name for my daughter. And so the little girl of my dreams came to be known as Somer and she was born at the exact moment Hurricane Bonnie made landfall near High Island, Texas.

Following the birth of Somer, my life took a different turn and became a small hurricane in and of itself. We moved from the land of the astronauts and water to Indianapolis, Indiana...the corporate headquarters for Larry's job. Although this was a huge promotion, Larry became very unhappy in Indiana as he missed the water and disliked the cold winters and it became my fault. And it was my fault. You see, the president of his company asked me if I would like to move closer to my family in Ohio and I said yes, and with that ammunition he convinced Larry to take the promotion. It put a wedge of sorts in our marriage and he spent more time away from me and Ryan and Somer, although he loved them dearly. I found part-time employment as a pre-school teacher where I could take my children as I could not bear to be separated from them. As sometimes happens with small children, they became my life and Larry became the intruder. As his company grew into bankruptcy our marriage did as well until finally there was no work for him and not much of a relationship for us either. In a last ditch effort to save what was left of our marriage, we decided to move to Clearwater, Florida, with no jobs...only our savings. You might be thinking this was a huge mistake. But there are no mistakes. We rented a house on a peninsula outside of Clearwater, but Larry could not find a job. I spent my time making the house a home, unpacking, and walking on eggshells so as not to start another argument. But there will be more about this later.

CERRILLOS, NEW MEXICO – NOVEMBER 27, 2011
OLD WINDMILL TRAIL

It was a Sunday afternoon and my cell phone was ringing and took my attention away from the painting I was working on in the studio. It was Somer and I had one of those gut-wrenching feelings. Two weeks ago, I spoke with Larry and could barely recognize his voice. "It is happening really quickly, Hon," he said. "Well, till death do us part," and handed the phone back to Ryan as I could not understand anything else he said. Ryan moved to Kansas City, Kansas and had been caring for his father and his half-brother Tyler since the first of September, when he was told of his father's terminal cancer. Tyler was a senior in high school and his mother had passed away several years ago, due to an overdose of prescription medication. She was involved in a car accident and was left with severe injuries. Larry gained custody of him many years prior to her passing. After searching all other options, it became clear there was no hope, and Larry decided to spend his final days at home. A Catholic hospice was called in to help. Somer was working in Denver and flew to Kansas whenever she could and Larry felt better when she was with him. And our children made peace with their father.

Somer said, "he is not responding to the meds, Mom. They always helped him before." "Call the hospice, Honey," I said. "Call them right now." I quit painting for the day and waited for the next call which came several hours later. "He's gone, Mom. Oh, Dad is gone. Hospice came and a priest was called in and he played guitar music and Dad just went to sleep," she sobbed. "Oh, I am so sorry, Honey... so sorry. How are Ryan and Tyler?" I said. "Mom, Ryan can't come to the phone right now. He will call you later." It would be several weeks before Ryan was able to call me, so severe was his grief. "I'll call you tomorrow, Mom," Somer told me.

People come into your life and touch you briefly and some stay for many years, as did Larry. It is the form we miss, I know, but this does not make it any easier. It is all part of the Grand Illusion. We "appear" to be born and we "appear" to die...but the spirit lives for eternity. And we will meet again, if we choose. But I miss that Ohio drawl of his.

MEW MEXICO–MARCH 2012
OLD WINDMILL TRAIL

I don't know what to expect as I haven't seen my son in many months. They both recently went through a horrible experience for ones so young as they and needed to get away for awhile. The Catholic hospice nurse was so impressed that she wrote a long article about her time spent with the two young men and it was published in the Kansas Catholic newsletter. Tyler continued to attend high school at Larry's insistence and also placed fourth in the state wrestling tournament. He did it for his father he said.

They came in my door smiling and both of them towering over me with their 6′ 3″ bodies and Tyler the spitting image of Larry. There was no mistaking they were brothers. "Hi Momma Doo," Ryan said. I had not seen Tyler in several years, yet it was as though we spoke yesterday. And they hiked and ate and slept and the peacefulness of the land and the animals helped them to heal. They stayed but a few days and were gone and back to Kansas, back to high school.

Tyler finished high school and started college in the fall. Ryan was left with the task of selling his father's two houses, one in Kansas and one in Clearwater. He would live in Kansas City for over another year before returning to The Land of Enchantment and to his home, to New Mexico.

Chapter Four

I am always within a whisper of your thoughts.
I am the very air you breathe.
Remember, take the next step...
one foot in front of the other.

CERRILLOS, NEW MEXICO – DECEMBER 1997
GOLDMINE ROAD

I am alone in a small one-room cabin, containing a finished basement, with no running water or gas or electric, which is not unusual within this area of Santa Fe County. Water is obtained by driving into the village of Cerrillos and drinking tea with an elderly woman who gives me tokens to use at the communal well to obtain water. How crazy is this??...yet the accepted norm here. A water tank is placed in the back of our truck, filled at the communal well, and brought back to the cabin. The fireplace is unsafe so we are currently using two propane heaters...one for the main room and one for the basement where Ryan and Somer's bedrooms are located. Surprisingly, they both actually like living in the cabin and are beginning to adjust to their new life in New Mexico. The dryer does not work, but the washing machine is functional, and a clothesline is used for drying. This is not an easy task to do in the wintertime, however the tiny cabin is located across the dirt road of the building site of our new house which makes the location so convenient. It is a Saturday afternoon and the snow begins to fall. Andy drove to Los Alamos to spend the weekend selling ghillie suits, our only source of income, which is primarily executed by me as he is busy building our new home. (Ghillie suits are camouflage suits used by the law enforcement and military which enables one to enter dangerous situations unnoticed.) Ryan and Somer are spending a few weeks over the Christmas vacation with their father in Los Angeles. I am sitting on a couch in front of an empty fireplace and my mind drifts back to the last eight years living in Zanesville.

ZANESVILLE, OHIO – 1991

Nineteen years had gone by so quickly. Although I visited my family frequently, flying in for holidays, from wherever...New York, Texas, Indiana, and now driving from Florida, moving back to my hometown after being absent for nineteen years, was quite a challenge to say the least. Yet new beginnings usually are that way. My children and I moved in with my parents after leaving, and finally divorcing their father, Larry, in Clearwater, Florida. The divorce was not a simple task to achieve due to my taking our children across the state line to Zanesville. I remember the day perfectly.

CLEARWATER, FLORIDA – JUNE 27, 1990

It was June 27, 1990, the day after Somer's fourth birthday. Our plan to start all over again, forget about his affairs and my lack of love, live on credit cards and savings until Larry found a job, had not quite worked out as planned. And the fighting and arguments began again, as they had in Indiana. Thoughts came frequently to simply leave, but I did not have the courage until this day. He was invited to go with a friend on a boat and needed get away from me, I am certain. But before he left, he began yelling loudly and I became afraid. The last time it happened this way, I was knocked down to the floor. He said I should find a job and that it was my turn to work. He was correct in his thinking, although I had worked several part-time jobs the last seven years, it should be me working now. The argument brought Ryan into the room and he was crying and telling his father to leave Mommy alone. Larry stormed out of the house and we could not remember if he said he would be gone for two hours or two days.

I comforted Ryan, who was still sobbing and sat down to think for a moment, but my heart was pounding and my brain racing. Then "out of the mouths of babes" my six-year-old son said, "Mommy, you need to call Me-Maw." I did. My mother said to come home. I woke up Somer, who was thankfully napping, grabbed a few clothes and toys, my jewelry, and my precious cat Ki-Ki, and with fourteen dollars and a credit card, drove to my hometown, Zanesville, Ohio. I left behind a beautiful house situated within a peninsula, surrounded by beautiful water, and filled with beautiful families. I left behind all of my worldly possessions, however in my possession was that which meant the most to me...my children and my cat. As my mother mentioned, I could have gone to a shelter and demanded half of everything, yet I chose an easier path for me...not so easy a path for my parents.

ZANESVILLE, OHIO – 1991

It was quite an adjustment for all concerned, as my parents were used to their solitude and not two children, myself and my cat. But I was so grateful to have a place to live. Ryan started the first grade and Somer was enrolled in a pre-school, so I could search for employment. Larry began to send a little money every week, however I sold every piece of jewelry I owned to stay afloat. Finally a part-time job came to me... painting animals and cars and motorcycles or anything anybody wished to see on sweatshirts at a store located within the Zanesville Mall. Sitting outside the store and painting several days a week was not for me, yet, at this moment, it was so much better than nothing. Finally a phone call came from a company known as 5 B's, an embroidery company, and they needed an artist!!! And could I come for an interview? And I got the job!!! Although the pay was minimal, health insurance for myself and my children was included. And life was good again. I continued my job painting sweatshirts while watching television with Ryan and Somer at night, and worked my day job as well. On Saturdays I cleaned my parents house and visited my childhood friend, Vicki, and her daughter, Lyndsay. Our children played together as we caught up on each other's lives. Both of us were divorced so we had much in common as we had experienced throughout all of our lives. We were friends since birth as our parents were friends also, and we went to grade school together and roomed together in college.

Within nine months a tiny house was rented and I was finally on my own, learning what it was like to be a single parent and attempting to fit in with the people in the town. It was not easy, accustomed as I was to living in large cities and not the slower pace of a small town where everyone knew everyone else. Eventually as the job painting sweatshirts was no longer a necessary income, my children became involved in soccer, dancing lessons, basketball, gymnastics, art lessons, etc. Isn't it wonderful how the universe always takes care of you that way? And the best gift, received two years later, was a house of my own, located in an old, yet well kept neighborhood across the street from the school my children attended! A few dates here and there were fun, but there was so little time. I was happy and not in need of a companion anyway. At least this is what I told myself. Holidays were filled with family...my parents, my brother Ken, his wife Denise, and my nephews Derek and Marcus. My brother and father spent much quality time with Ryan and Somer, helping to fill the void of an absent parent, although they visited with Larry over Christmas vacation and for a month during the summertime. My father never missed any game of any sport Ryan and Somer participated in.

I was driven to succeed at my job...choosing to acquire more money to support my children, and also intensely disliked taking orders from anyone. As 5 B's grew into a large corporation my promotions grew as well, until I was promoted to the position of Creative Artist, with an office of my own. And within a year, another promotion. I became the Art Director and no more taking orders. 5 B's was expanding into retail and were manufacturing their own sweatshirts embroidered with my designs on them. It was a family-owned business which began in their basement, and although now millionaires, they were very, very nice people to work for.

A Creative Art department was required, with new artists to hire, and I was going to embark on a new adventure. It was like living a dream, one which I asked for many years ago. (Always remember to ask. If it is asked from the heart, it is given. Always.) Several of the layout artists joined the new department and the process of interviewing began. One of the artists I interviewed remains a friend of mine to this day. Her name is Karen, and she brought the most beautiful portfolio to the interview. I simply "knew" her. (Later in my life I learned through my psychic dowser friend Bryan, that we had been sisters in the same Anasazi tribe and when I was killed by a mountain lion...afterwards she raised my daughter.) She had been working as a graphic designer illustrating fashion, with models wearing the most beautiful clothing, however she added something unique in her illustrations...animals peeking out of handbags or held in arms. She was hired on the spot. When Karen began working we ate lunch together, something I had not ever done with anyone else...choosing always to be alone with my thoughts. We were kindred spirits of sorts and she knew the spiritual side of life long before it came to me.

It was about this time that Andy made his dramatic entrance into my life and as you know change occurred almost instantaneously. Soon, after returning from our wedding in Las Vegas, my parents decided to sell their home and move to Albuquerque. My father recently retired from his job at a local bank, following 43 years of employment. My mother, who was well known throughout Ohio for her artistic endeavors, winning awards of the highest, desired a change of scenery. And they left. Within several months my mother began to speak to me on the phone of attending monthly sessions and listening to a woman who channeled the Archangel Gabriel. "You must visit us. You must have a private session with Him," she said.

That August, Ryan and Somer and I took our first vacation together alone and flew to Albuquerque! I fell head over heels in love with the blue skies and the magical beauty of the Land of Enchantment. My private session with the woman who channeled Gabriel changed my entire outlook on life. For the first time, I felt unconditional love and it was emanating from this being. Dabbling in tarot cards, reading about witchcraft, and feeling and hearing spirits who had passed was nothing compared to this. I was told I am a "worker of the light." I began to wake up. It was time. No more would the world seen through the physical eyes be "my" world. There was an entire universe filled with life, and universes beyond this one, and angels and ascended masters and nature spirits and on and on. I returned to the land of the rolling hills and green grass and overcast skies, a changed woman. My mother began to send me tapes of the monthly group sessions with Gabriel and I learned of the year 2012 and of earth changes and the Great Awakening.

Andy had been a member of the Theosophical Society in his

younger years, an organization formed to advance spiritual principles and search for truth, and also spent time with Peace Pilgrim following her around the country as she spoke about peace and faith and worked her miracles. Along with listening to the tapes of Gabriel, I conversed with Andy. A friend of mine at 5 B's, whose name was Carol, asked to hear the tapes and we decided to form a group, and had a "Gathering" once a month to discuss "the spiritual side of life" and the year 2012. (Although not known to me at that time, we are already spiritual beings, having an Earthly experience.) My friend Karen and two other women, plus Andy, made up our little group. As time passed and with a changed focus, I began to hear voices and feel touches and see glimpses into the higher dimensions. (Here, I must make mention of the "touches." At first it felt as though an angel was touching my hand, but when the touching moved to other parts of my body, I knew whoever was doing this was no angel and I told it to go away. It did, but Andy's sword lying under our bed allowed me to feel safe.) As my consciousness grew, my perception of the physical world changed even more.

Andy decided to quit his job as an elementary school teacher and started his own ghillie suit business. My friend Carol quit her job at 5 B's and started working for him and went back to college. I yearned to have more time or any time at all to paint. Feeling compelled to do so, eventually I also quit my job at 5 B's and started working with Andy as his business was thriving. Again, you might be thinking this was a mistake. And again, there are none.

When Andy decided to take a partner, I knew it was the wrong decision on the physical plane yet spiritually it was an old Karma that needed to be worked through and balanced. The man who became his partner, David, well, he was simply untrustworthy...at least to me. Soon thereafter my salary was taken away and the money made by the ghillie suit company which had been substantial, was now controlled by David and simply disappeared. After several months I convinced Andy to check the joint bank account and over $40,000 was not accounted for and an attorney was consulted. The next evening, and because of the advice from our attorney, we confiscated everything out of the building rented for sewing and assembling the ghillie suits. A court date followed, yet David was adept when it came to embezzlement and so the equipment and supplies were divided and the company dissolved. However we continued to make the suits for several more years.

At this time my mother was contemplating the idea of purchasing some land outside of cities to become self-sufficient in order to survive the impending earth changes...with land to plant gardens and become independent of the grid system. She invited us to become a part of her plan. Another trip to New Mexico ensued. The following summer we all flew to Albuquerque to visit my parents and search for this "place." We found eighty acres of beautiful juniper-covered land on Goldmine Road, about twenty-four miles south of Santa Fe. And another beginning began. Although my brother and his family were asked to come as well, he declined and stayed in Ohio. My house sold in three months and we left with Ryan and Somer, and our three cats, for the land which held so much magic for me.

My brother, Ken, and his wife, Denise, came the last night before we departed to say their "good-byes" as Andy and I were about to move the washer up the steep flight of basement steps. Perfect timing. Their help was much appreciated, but before they left Ken said to me, "Are you sure you want to do this, Karin?" "It's too late now, Ken. It's already done."

ZANESVILLE, OHIO – 1957 AND BEYOND

"I'm coming," she said as we silently walked back to the bedroom I shared with him...he on the top bunk, me on the bottom one. (In later years they told me that I stood in their bedroom and stared until she awoke.) "Another dream," she said as she talked him back to sleep. My baby brother had nightmares from a distance past and only my mother could make him calm down, make it all right again for him. The horrible screaming stopped.

The Sagittarian horse and the Taurus bull locked horns throughout our childhood. Ornery and mean were adjectives used to describe him. A rat, he was. Total opposites, we were. He the outgoing athlete, and me the quiet artist/dancer. He was a nemesis of sorts to me, although following the footsteps of a "good girl" sister all through grade school must have been difficult for him. "Your sister was an excellent student," they told him. "You have much to do to keep up with her," they said. How wrong were they? Those teachers?

But he was quick, a fast runner, smart, able to leap tall buildings, I thought silently...a pitcher for the baseball team, a quarterback for the football team. We all watched him succeed. Together we played cowboys and Indians, rode bicycles, and sleds on trails with ramps that took us up so high we could touch the sun. We rolled down the green, grass covered hills, caught bumble bees and lightning bugs in glass jars, and fought great battles sitting upon huge inner tubes at the lake. When he said, "Come play football with me, Karin. We need another one. Get up and do something." I did. When we shared a pizza in high school and developed food poisoning, we bonded. When he threw himself into his dresser and broke his teeth during one of his nightmares, we bonded. And when I left for college I missed him terribly...my brother, Ken.

Now so busy are we both with our lives and our families...living so far apart. I miss his intense energy, his laughter and his jokes, and the sound of his voice saying, "come play football with me, Karin. Get up and do something."

Chapter Five

Focus within the Divine Source as you write.
Do not be hesitant of repeating your otherworldly experiences.
Release this to Me.
Hold true to your beliefs and be unafraid
of that which forms within this reality.

HOPEWELL, OHIO – 1972

"Kay, look at that plane. It seems to be following us. I'm going to slow down and see what happens," I said to my friend with laughter in my voice. As I slowed my Volkswagen bug down to forty-five miles per hour, the "plane" or "light" maintained the same pace. "Maybe it's a flying saucer," I said to her, but Kay was not amused. As I drove faster, it followed suit. When I slowed down, it did the same, and I knew it was not an airplane, it was a craft from another world.

"You're freaking me out, Karin," Kay said, "just get me home!" We were driving from the "No Place," a club in Newark, Ohio, where there were bands and dancing and lots of boys, taking Route 40 to her house in Hopewell. There were no other cars on the highway and it was around 1:30 AM. As soon as I pulled into her driveway, the spacecraft disappeared, and she ran into her house. I do not remember the rest of the drive home.

CERRILLOS, NEW MEXICO – DECEMBER 1997
GOLDMINE ROAD

The snowfall was quite beautiful as it covered the cactus, and the mountains became a blur in the distance. How wonderful! Complete silence, until the tiny cabin began to leak droplets of water onto the wooden floor. Pots and pans were placed under the leaks and I returned to the couch as the drops continued...drip, drip, drip...and fell asleep for a moment, awaking to the nudge of a very, very tall man. His head almost reached the ceiling as he looked down at me wearing a red shirt and black pants, with tall black boots almost up to his knees. I knew this man...I knew the unique bone structure about his forehead, the dark eyes and pale complexion...his energy was familiar. I was able to maintain eye contact until the vision was gone, however the look on his face will not be forgotten. For weeks I felt as though I was experiencing a new love, walking upon the stars... and mentioned nothing of this to Andy.

A few weeks later during a private session with the woman who channeled Gabriel in Albuquerque, his name was revealed. It was Andor. Gabriel told me he came from Andromeda, a galaxy approximately 2.5 million light years away. He was a soul mate with whom I made a contract. The Andromedans used my DNA and a set of twins were the result...a girl and a boy who were hybrids on another planet. There will be more children Gabriel informed me, from other galaxies, as my consent had been given to other extraterrestrial races to take DNA for their hybrid children project, prior to my entrance into this plane of existence. You may think this extraterrestrial visitation would have shocked me to my deepest core, yet it did not.

My DNA would (along with many others) be used to help save the forms of other extraterrestrial races which were dying, due to procreation within their races only and/or due to (my opinion) reliance on technology. They needed Earth human's DNA to survive...to kind of jump start their races. As they began to fade, technology was used in some instances as a "cure." Some lost their hearts, their emotions. They simply forgot. (And again... my opinion at that time.) They began to notice the beings upon Earth and the full range of emotions. They remembered and desired that which is taken for granted here. And as we are all one, I gave my consent. Sounds simple, doesn't it? I felt as though I was in two places at the same time...walking within a narrow path and not certain of, or even aware of, my next step.

Our stay within the tiny cabin was brief yet memorable. And although we all experienced great sadness when our beloved eight-year-old cat Ki-Ki had to be put down, we were all pleased with the move. My wish to be a "stay-at-home" kind of mom was granted and I sewed the ghillie suits within a tiny space located behind the bathroom. Andy continued building our new house, along with a construction crew, which was being financed by my father. The money accrued at the sale of my house in Zanesville had slowly dwindled due to the enormous rent of the cabin and the cost of the move.

Somer was the first to arrive home from school and I picked her up at the bottom of Goldmine Road and so enjoyed our time together until she made a new friend, Coral, who was my daughter from a past life. One who did not stay long, so I was told. She would remain Somer's best friend through high school.

In middle school Somer experienced problems with gangs who also rode home on the school bus. She was very pretty, petite, with long blonde hair. The boys loved her, but the girls were jealous. It did not help that she did not look Hispanic at all, and I was forced to speak with the principal, who assured me the bullying would stop immediately. It did not. Even Ryan and his tall basketball friends could not prevent this from occurring. Finally, I remembered Ryan's middle school basketball coach, who was Hispanic himself. Upon meeting Ryan and Somer, myself and Andy, when we first arrived, he said Ryan would have no problem "fitting in." Ryan was extremely tall, with black hair and dark features. He looked like everyone else. But he told me if Somer ever had any problems to let him know, and he would take care of it. I called him that very day, and two days later Somer was able to ride the bus again.

Ryan was quick to adjust to his new life and became a member of the eighth grade basketball team and also made a new friend, John. They went through college together and continue to be friends to this day.

In May, we moved into the newly built, yet not quite finished, house on Goldmine Road, directly across the road from the cabin. Andy continued building, only this time it was my parents house, a short distance away. I continued to sew the ghillie suits, painted, and maintained my status of a "stay-at-home" mom. Vegetable gardens were planted outside and plants of all sorts grew within my house. Sunflowers in large pots covered my kitchen floors...geraniums abounded in many windows.

I looked forward to each day, waking early to meditate before cooking breakfast for everyone and seeing my children off to school. The sound of laughter and video games and teenage noise filled the house on weekends. My parent's home was completed and they moved from Albuquerque and began their new life on the mountain. My mother continued to attend the monthly sessions with Gabriel and see her friends from Albuquerque and Dad played golf weekly and attended the local breakfast club gatherings where new homes and alternative energy were displayed and discussed. I must tell you how utterly and totally happy was I at this time of my life. Anything planted within the ground or inside pots grew and flourished. Yet after a few years a sense of unease began to envelope me.

Time moved by quickly and as my love for animals began to expand we adopted a puppy named Nikky who became a delight to all of us. Thirty-one baby chicks were also purchased from the local feed store. They lived in my art studio for several months within a large heated cage. I thoroughly enjoyed cleaning their cage twice a day and giving them vegetables and talking with them, holding them...so sweet they were as only baby chicks can be. Until one day, the roosters began to fly around the studio and it was time to take them outside to live in their newly built coop. All were named, but the star of the flock was Mr. Bob...an ornery rooster. My mother came frequently to see the chickens and taught Mr. Bob how to crow. He listened and learned. He especially loved to be the first rooster to stand outside Somer's bedroom window and crow loudly, just to hear her open her window and shout obscenities at him. We now had Nikky, two cats named Annie and Montgomery, and the thirty-one chickens. They all taught me to love even more.

As the eggs arrived from our laying chickens, so did many neighbors. Not only did they come to see the chickens, as they were quite beautiful, they also came for the eggs. Bryan the dowser came frequently to chat and offer advice, yet only when asked for. He came with a smile and a joke and we talked. Eventually I learned of his intuitive nature and psychic abilities. One day he mentioned seeing glimpses of a young woman wearing a pink dress. I too, saw portions of her dress while walking Nikky early in the mornings. He suggested I connect with her to help her move into the Light...and I did...connect with her, that is.

The Lady in pink "showed" me her story. She and her husband had a mining claim on our property, many years ago, and they were struggling to stay alive, suffering many hardships such as lack of food and fighting the elements. One day, several men rode up on horseback, killed her husband and raped and killed her as well. She did not know why she could not leave and was still trapped between worlds. My suggestion to look for the Light of God was answered in silence, and I rarely saw her afterwards.

Several months later, Bryan stopped by and asked where my daughter was going, "all dressed up?" "My daughter is not here Bryan," I said. "Well thar she is," he said and pointed. "But there is nothing there," and a thought occurred to me. "What is she wearing?" "A pink dress," he said, and the at same moment we knew who she was. It was the "Lady in Pink" as she came to be known to us. "I never saw one of them in their entire form, like this," he said. It was the first time, but as you may recall there was soon to be another instance in the near future when we both saw one in their entire form...the medicine man on top of the "Sacred Hill."

Listening to the tapes of Gabriel, discussing them with Mom, attending some group sessions, having my own private sessions, and meditating almost daily, enabled my consciousness to expand and my eyes began to "see" more into other dimensions. I began to hear voices from beyond the veil quite clearly and experience the most vivid dreams of being aboard extraterrestrial spacecraft or visiting other planets. Andy and I spoke with God, or the Prime Source, daily. I asked questions and wrote the information as it came through Andy, and we have volumes of material from these sessions. One morning before meditating I saw the light body of the master Kuthumi. He manifested as bright golden and bronze sparkles of light as he walked past me. Once my grandmother came through Andy and she said, "be a part of this world, yet be as an observer... apart from it." Later that evening her light body appeared to me. It was a magnificent sight to see for I had missed her so when she departed! Her light body was sparkles of golden light, about six feet high.

On another occasion I experienced a huge "awakening" of sorts, and felt the most loving and profound God energy. For days I saw in my mind a pulsation, a swirling white light of male and female energy... and breathed in and out with the pulsing of this great loving energy. Afterwards, I became so happy and in love with life and walked around with a smile on my face at all times. As you can imagine, living with me was not easy during this time. The voices from beyond the veil became so loud I began writing everything down. Many from the other side wished to speak with me and at times a hum of voices could be heard. Maintaining this sense of peace and love was not an easy task within this world of duality, and regretfully after several months, it began to fade, although not totally. The dreams continued.

One of the dreams involved being onboard a Zeti Reticuli spacecraft, filled with deformed hybrid babies. Myself and other women were holding and comforting these small beings. At that time it was not apparent whether any of them were from my DNA, but a very disturbing dream it was. Many of us, as previously mentioned, contracted to give our DNA to promote saving the extraterrestrial races from extinction. Earth has long been known as the "melting pot" for a good reason. Other worldly races have come and gone and left their seeds behind, so to speak. You could say we are all aliens.

On another occasion I dreamed of going to a planet, known to me as Aldebron. (Later in years I learned the planet was actually a higher dimension known as Avalon.) It was filled with animals unknown to Earth, large bodies of water, and plants and trees that were able to communicate with humans. The entire planet seemed to be completely covered green with vegetation that was so alive and in motion.

I awoke one evening late at night to find myself on the couch in the living room. I felt a strange sensation of "feeling" my "son" yet my brain said to me, "he, my son Ryan, is asleep in his bedroom." Glancing at the television set there appeared a small brown humanoid form. (At times I see them in full color, and sometimes they appear in a brown tinge and this one was brown.) It was not in front of it, not behind it. It was as if the television was not there at all. The head was oval shaped and the neck was extremely thin. The body was very short and I thought, it is a boy and he is telling me he is my son! And in an instant, he was gone. I wish I had been more responsive to him. I wish I had said, "come to me, let me get to know you, let me love you." But I did not. The next morning Andy mentioned a dream he had during the night, in which I gave birth to a boy, from another planetary system.

I began to view our Earth, (due to the acquired knowledge I had at the time) to be what is known as "the nursery of the souls" and believe that some of us came here to learn and to grow, to enrich our souls, and to assist others wherever needed. I did both. I believe the calling came to me, and yet the knowledge within my beingness has expanded beyond all expectations. Do I like it? At times...brief times... I learned to do the dance of life...such a magnificent gift from our Creator. Fondness for this illusion had grown to the point that I now must remember who and what I AM, and where I came from. Some call us star seeds, some call us light workers, some crazy...yet all heard the call to come.

My paintings began to change as the forms of my hybrid children filled the canvases. To anyone but me, they appeared as Earth humans...yet they were not. Of course there was a genetic connection to them, however the paintings simply flowed out of me. When a canvas was finished I asked their names and they answered me. They were from the Pleiades, Avalon, Andromeda, and others whose names have been forgotten. The color schemes were not realistic, yet all had perfect features. A friend, whom I was about to meet, simply loved my new work.

One autumn afternoon while working in my garden, a man drove down the driveway with a load of gravel. Andy had told me about him. His name was Greg and he owned the Cerrillos Gravel Yard. He was tall and slender and wore a cowboy hat, which he took off when I introduced myself. Quite charming, I thought, and with those bright blue eyes he was quite handsome too. "My partner Ann would just love you" he said. We made plans to get together and she did "just love me," and I just loved her. She was twelve years my senior with golden blonde hair and green eyes, and a loud distinctive voice and laugh. Although barely five feet in height, she had a presence that, at times, overpowered the love of her life...Greg.

They would simply drop by to see us when she returned home from working at her restaurant in Santa Fe. Many Sundays, Andy and I would visit with them. During one of their visits, I finally got up the courage to tell them I was a vegetarian. Greg said, "well, you eat vegetables, don't you? And you have to kill them before you eat them, don't you? What's the difference?" He was absolutely correct.

Together, Ann and Greg shared their home and their hearts with whomever came within their presence. Greg was a "Renaissance man" of sorts and could converse on almost any topic with anyone. He never refused to help another...whether it was a vehicle that needed repair, towed, or dug out of a ditch, or a friend that needed a place to stay. Ann loved cooking, gardening, pitching horseshoes (well they both did) and people. Their trailer was always filled with the smell of something wonderful cooking. She experimented with new ways of gardening and would say "you just have to see this plant," before I could sit down. They threw the most fantastic parties, usually when there was a horseshoe pitch, but also every New Year's Day.

At one of their gatherings I met a woman named Marilyn, who had mesmerizing bright blue eyes and joy simply spilled out of her body. She was one I recognized from the distant past...life that is. She has a rare gift of speaking with the voice of God. Over time we became friends and still are to this day. Ann and Marilyn and myself formed a triad of sorts and met every Saturday for what came to be known as a "beer picnic." Together we discussed our problems, concerns, our husbands or boyfriends, our children, or whatever. Yet it was just the three of us and all others were excluded. This lasted for several years until a tragedy occurred. But more on that later.

You may be wondering about my parents who lived a few hundred feet away. Dad came often to visit and we took a walk daily, attended Ryan's basketball games and track meets, and Somer's baseball games and track meets as well. Mom was more of a loner, choosing her privacy to paint, listening to Art Bell on the radio, or tapes of the

Gabriel sessions. Although she also visited and we all celebrated holidays together.

Mom introduced me to two of her new friends she met at the sessions with the one who channeled the archangel Gabriel in Albuquerque. The mother's name was Pat, and her daughter Leslie. Upon several occasions, Mom and I drove to have tea with Pat and some of her metaphysical friends. She lived in a small town north of Santa Fe known as El Dorado. The conversations were always interesting and enlightening, and the food delicious.

One day at tea, sitting at the tiny wooden table were Leslie, Pat, Mom, myself, and a new woman Pat recently met. I do not recall her name, however she was a tarot card reader and a psychic and was currently building a new house nearby. She asked to do a reading for all of us, although Leslie wisely refused. Mom, Pat, and I drew negative, and I mean really negative cards, except for one. We all had the card which represented the Archangel Gabriel... perhaps for protection. Following a charming bit of tea and snacks we decided to drive to see the new woman's "house in progress."

All was going exceedingly well until she took us for a walk outside to stand upon an energy vortex, as she called it. She beckoned me to stand on it first and as I did the energy shot up my legs and straight to my stomach and heart, and I sank to the ground. A sensation of heat was felt around my neck and shoulders, as the woman described seeing a medicine man behind me healing my body. I felt the presence of an elderly woman and another man nearby (they were my mother and husband from a previous life) as the stranger woman began to speak of that past life...one in which I died from an attack by a mountain lion. A young daughter and husband who dearly loved me were left behind. We were members of an Anasazi tribe. Is this beginning to sound familiar? (It was the same lifetime Bryan the dowser would bring to my attention years later) "A friend you know very well was your sister that lifetime and she raised your daughter who is your daughter again this lifetime," she said. "Do you know who the sister is?" she inquired. Instantly I knew as tears came to my eyes. She is my artist friend Karen, from Ohio, whom I worked with at the 5 B's embroidery company.

After several moments and with the assistance of Leslie's arm I was able to stand. No one spoke. Perfect silence. I felt as if all of my energy was drained from my body and my stomach still ached with pain. Shortly thereafter Mom and I departed for home on the mountain. Pat refused to see the stranger woman again. Although unaware at the time, I now know I had been psychically attacked, but was left with a rare gift...a glimpse into the past. One that had affected this lifetime as you will see. I should have thanked the woman profusely.

Many changes were about to take place on the road known as Goldmine, within my home and family. Andy and I continued our daily talks with God and we knew something was about to happen. But what?

After the stress of helping with the construction of our house and my parents house, and working for the construction manager, Andy, who had been diagnosed with a 30% disability due to Post Traumatic Stress during the Viet Nam War, seemed to go through a transition. He became 100% disabled, and basically was told by the government that he would be paid 100% VA benefits not to work. It was a very difficult time for him and all those around him, for he would lose his temper and rant and rage for, what seemed to us, no good reason. On one hand, he no longer worked, but he was also not always comfortable to be around. The ghillie suit business took a turn for the worse, as our best customer, Peter from Germany, was accidentally shot while instructing a class. Peter became a paraplegic and it would be quite awhile until he was able to recover and begin placing orders from us again.

Ryan was a junior at the Santa Fe High School and a starter for the varsity basketball team. Although going through all of the trials and tribulations and mood swings of a typical teenager, he seemed to be doing quite well. He made my heart sing and my soul dance.

Somer was not adjusting as well to high school. And suddenly calls came informing me she was skipping classes, or late for classes, or skipping the entire day all together. Several of her teachers informed me that she was so intelligent she could teach the classes herself. Coral, her best friend, was living with us for several months following the divorce of her parents. She seemed to help Somer, but eventually Coral left us to live with her father, and Somer was alone until she met Jason. A senior, I was told. The Homecoming King, I was told. Too old for her, I thought, but he was so very nice and respectful. And life continued smoothly...for awhile.

The uneasy feeling within me began to expand as I watched my mother grow increasingly unhappy and I knew great changes would soon come to my peaceful kingdom. It was during this time of uncertainty that another unworldly experience occurred. I fell asleep on our couch in the living room one evening and woke up to see a tall man with black hair, wearing a long white robe, standing across the room from me. He emanated a brilliant golden light. I stared at him until he disappeared, and in the morning mentioned him to Andy. That was Jesus, also known as Yeshua, he told me, as chills ran down my arms and legs. Later that day I heard a voice say to me, "why? Why did you not go with your Brother?" To this day it still puzzles me why I did nothing but stare at him without recognition.

My mother did not seem to fit into life on the mountain, and did not make new friends, although she had many friends in Albuquerque. She so missed the city life filled with galleries and restaurants and exciting people to meet. She decided to sell the property, and move back to Albuquerque. And my father agreed.

ZANESVILLE, OHIO – 1954 AND BEYOND

She was beautiful and tall (at least to me) and when going out to parties she wore a purple and blue dress, covered in rhinestones. Her eyes were dark brown, almost black, that twinkled when she laughed. My mother. How could she be so pretty I asked as a small child? How could she be so smart? And I did my best to please her, My mother, my Mom.

Her first painting was of me...a five-year-old child in a red frilly dress, sitting upon a chair of light. How special was I?

She took me to dance lessons when I was thought to be shy. She sewed my costumes. And I was good. They all said so. She was proud of the little girl in the red frilly dress. She drove me to art lessons every Saturday and afterwards we would go to auctions in search of precious things.

In high school, she sewed the most beautiful clothes for me, majorette costumes and Homecoming attendant suits. She watched over my boyfriends who were more afraid of her than my father. In college she bought me a TV set, when I had none. When I got pregnant and he wouldn't marry me, she said, "I can do it, " and she did, and he did... marry me, that is. My mother. My Mom.

And as years went by and she looked back, she thought she may have fought too many battles for me. I say she is wrong. I say all that mattered was that she cared and loved me enough to want to help me. My mother. My Mom.

A wise woman once said "it is as it is." And it is that I chose my parents well. What have we been to each other in past lives? Have I been their parents too? Is this our last lifetime together? Will we get off the rollercoaster and take the ferris wheel to the top and climb the rainbow steps to the stars, to Avalon and beyond? This I do not know. Yet if we do I hope we do it together. My mother. My Mom. My friend.

CERRILLOS, NEW MEXICO – 2001
GOLDMINE ROAD

Once informed of the changes that were about to take place, a normally quiet, peaceful me released that which is known as the "Worden Temper." (Worden was Grandmother's maiden name) And I caused a rift in the relationship held so close to my heart with my parents.

Feeling compelled to move with my husband, my children and cats to New Mexico, selling my house and changing my life to live with my parents on the same property had been an enormous undertaking for all of us. I truly believed that we all would remain together for many years, but this was not to be. I should have reminded myself that all is in Divine Order. There can be nothing less than this. We would all take separate paths as you will soon see.

Chapter Six

Remain strong during this time...
as you believe, so shall it be.
This IS My Decree.

CERRILLOS, NEW MEXICO – 2002
GOLDMINE ROAD

We continued to live in our home, yet I felt as if I were on "pins and needles" as they say, waiting for a call from a realtor to spring into action. With two teenagers, a dog and two cats, cleaning was a required necessity for every one of their visits. These were extremely trying times for me. My daughter begged me to allow her to drop out of high school, and with the chaos surrounding me, I finally granted her wish on one condition. She must be home-schooled and take her classes online. She must also pay for the courses, which she did. As you might suspect, this did not work out well. She enjoyed her job working at a restaurant in Santa Fe and spent her free time with her boyfriend Jason, who was now a freshman at the University of New Mexico. Eventually Somer asked to move into an apartment with Jason. I was sewing ghillie suits (due to Peter's recent recovery), cleaning constantly, and packing...for where, I knew not. So I allowed Somer to leave and she moved in with Jason.

Although unaware of it at the time, I now know we were both seeking a Karmic balance, for as you recall, the last lifetime spent together I left her much sooner than expected. (This type of a balancing act can continue over and over again, one lifetime after another unless it is recognized and discontinued...at least from my understanding) You must think me insane. You must think that I did not love my daughter. This is untrue. I loved her so much that I allowed her to make her own choices. She was also terribly convincing. The only stipulation was that she call me every day. And she did.

My heart ached with pain every time Dad walked over to our house to tell us more of what I considered to be bad news. (It was not so for him as he felt every step taken was closer to selling the property and releasing his guilt. I believe he felt guilt for giving me and my family so much, and not doing the same for my brother.) However, in retrospect, he did the best he could to make a semblance of peace. Ryan, who was a senior in high school and very busy, seemed always to be present whenever my father appeared and was such a comfort to me, even at such a young age. My mother refused any communication with either Andy or myself. Andy became enraged at times with frustration, and although not directed at me, it literally fell upon my shoulders. A great sadness set into my body.

After Somer left, one of my chickens, whose name was Little Dove, became paralyzed with a disease and had to be brought into the house and separated from the other chickens. I made her a bed in Somer's vacant bedroom. With the advice from a dear friend Leslie, a veterinarian, Little Dove fully recovered. But during her recovery, she made quite an impression on prospective buyers. She liked to show off a bit, demonstrating her newfound mobility by walking and clucking with joy. Although not many would have placed a chicken in their house while showing it to prospective buyers, the woman who enjoyed seeing Little Dove more than any purchased the house.

As time moved forward, our fears were replaced with acceptance... especially when our friend Peter from Germany gave us $20,000 to help us buy some land. Our dear friend Greg, who knew this area so well, told us of a property he thought we might consider. He drove us out the long and now so familiar dirt road to the land we now live upon. There was a pond of all things in the desert! And a windmill as well. And we had water! And the land was situated in a beautiful valley and all the mountain ranges in the area were visible. Soon thereafter we met with the realtor and purchased this magnificent land. Truly a gift from God! (As an aside, the moment I jumped out of Greg's truck and put my feet on the ground, I felt energy pouring into my body, as if the land was grateful for me.)

The spring and summer months of 2002 were spent making the ghillie suits and driving back and forth to our new property, preparing the foundation, building the new chicken coop, and cleaning our current home for prospective buyers. At some point, I quit painting and have no memory of why or when it happened. But there was now a focus. There was hope that all would work out perfectly.

Through all of this so-called chaos, my parents divorced after 50 years of marriage. My father became so distraught, my brother Ken arrived to drive him back to Zanesville. He left my mother everything within the house but also left her with the task of selling it as well. Within a year, my father married a wonderful woman whose name is Mary. As time was allowed to work its magic, my mother and I began to communicate again. I was so grateful, for she was and is my dearest friend.

Chapter Seven

Do not make your book a chore.
Make it a melody of sorts...a song.
Allow "it" to surround you and
step into the flow of your life.
Make the effort. Take the step. Finish the book.

CERRILLOS, NEW MEXICO – NOVEMBER 22, 2012
OLD WINDMILL TRAIL

It is the Saturday following Thanksgiving and my phone is singing and it reads "Somer." She must have landed. "Hi, Honey." "Hi, Mom, an hour flight to Denver is taking me five hours. Can you hear the slot machines? I'm in Vegas!" (She did all of this traveling just to come home.) "Mom, I read the six chapters from your book and it is sooo good I didn't want to put it down. I'm looking for the smoking lounge," she says while walking through the airport. I hear her ask several people where it is. "Mom, the book is so good. I read it twice on the flight. I want to edit it for you. I'm good at it and I'll do it. I'm really proud of you, Mom. It's not what you write it's all about how you write it. OK, Mom, I found it (the smoking lounge.) I'll call you tomorrow. Bye, Mom." The Golden Child works her magic once again and dances me back to my work. I began writing.

CERRILLOS, NEW MEXICO – 2002
OLD WINDMILL TRAIL ROAD

It seems that since moving to New Mexico my life has revolved around building houses and moving. Our house in the valley is nearing completion. Living in the tiny cold trailer within such a confined space is wearing on both Andy and myself. Our friend, Ken, who sold us the trailer and helped us move our remaining 15 chickens, also installed the solar system and assisted in the wiring and electrical work. He was an angel disguised in the body of an ex-Viet Nam engineer. How quickly and efficiently he moved, never missing a beat. "You look so tired, Karin. You have to get out of this trailer," he said. "You need a rest." But I cannot. Not yet.

An order for ghillie suits came from Peter and I gratefully took a break from the insulation and constant hammering, and began sewing. It is early winter and yet we are without heat so my sewing is executed at 50 degree temperatures, until all twelve suits are completed and shipped overseas.

Finally a wood burner is installed. March can be brutally cold in the valley as there is nothing to stop the wind as it blows with a hint of spring, and a promise of the end of winter.

One morning while cooking in the trailer, a spark ignited the stove on fire and I dashed into the house calling for Andy. He arrived with a fire extinguisher and we moved our cat Annie, our dog Nikky, and our mattress into the unfinished house. I laid down on the mattress with Annie in front of the wood burner and fell asleep while Andy drove into Santa Fe. I awoke four hours later when he returned and the house was cold and the fire out, so tired was I not to even notice. We adapted to cooking on the wood burner and living out of coolers filled with ice, until a refrigerator and stove were installed. This incident encouraged us to move at a faster pace, and we did. A final inspection was received in May, although the mudding and plaster work was unfinished.

The five horses and seven cows continued to stay with us and I looked forward to feeding them every morning and night. At times it became a sitcom of sorts as I learned to expect the unexpected with humor. A few of the horses were so wild they would not allow me to get within five feet of them. Yet I so enjoyed watching their antics and behavior. One morning Ci-Ci, the beautiful appaloosa, jumped over my body while feeding her because Nikky barked and startled her from the other side of the fence. I was kicked by Star several times, and bitten by Co-Co, the wild Mustang. The kicks were an accident, the bite was not. They taught me well, and I learned, yet the learning curve at times was brutal. But oh, how I loved it. Every minute of it.

One morning while feeding the horses, I noticed they were covered with the hail which had recently fallen from the sky... and it was now raining. Compassion welled up deep within my heart that they must be so terribly cold. I breathed in the God energy and breathed it out, and to my astonishment the sun shone so brightly it melted the ice from their backs. We built a windbreak for them that very day, and they were so very grateful. It could be seen in their eyes.

During that first year, Momacita gave birth to a beautiful calf we named Rafina. I searched and searched for Momacita when she left the tiny herd to be alone during the birthing process. She was found underneath a juniper tree, deep in the valley with the new little one that reminded me of a young fawn. Momacita left the Earth plane almost six months from the day her calf was born. Not knowing what to do, I contacted our veterinarian who asked me the age of the calf. Six months, I told him. She will be fine. Six months is exactly what she needs to be to survive without her mother's milk. And she did... survive, that is.

The next several months were spent finishing the walls. The dreaded mudding, taping, plastering and sanding had begun. Andy completed most of the drywall himself, and the rest was up to me. I attacked the job of plastering with little or no pleasure, finishing every room, until there was only a small area left in our bedroom to finish.

At this time I attended a private session in Albuquerque with the woman who channeled Gabriel. He strongly suggested that I stop working on the house immediately. He also asked why I had not been painting. I had been so trapped in the victim mode of life, working, working, working, not having any fun and forgot to play. Slowly, oh so slowly, I began to paint and to this day have not finished that section in my bedroom. Every year since, I have looked at it and plan to finish it, yet it has not occurred in eleven years.

Another huge order for ghillie suits came from Peter in Germany, and I sewed and sewed and completed the entire 25 suit order myself and decided to spend the entire profits myself. I had become "car-less" since before leaving Goldmine Road, and had to ask Andy to drive his truck every time I went anywhere. My beautiful green van had served me well when transporting my children and three cats from Ohio to New Mexico, but entirely useless upon our arrival to the wild west. For many years prior to leaving the land of the green rolling hills of Ohio, a red jeep had been my wish. It was my dream. And so, with my profits, I drove to a used car dealership in Santa Fe and informed the salesman I was interested in purchasing a jeep. "Actually a red Jeep." He looked at me strangely and said, "come with me." And to my astonishment a red Jeep Cherokee was backing out of a garage where it had been washed only a moment ago. "This came in last night," he told me. "It's yours," he said. And it was and still is. I named her Cherry and she loves the mud and the snow and the treacherous road and has taken good care of me for all of these years. She was definitely another gift from God.

CERRILLOS, NEW MEXICO – 2003 AND BEYOND
OLD WINDMILL TRAIL

The new year brought to me a new job. I began working part-time at the tiny Post Office in the village of Cerrillos. Although it was a huge learning experience, it was exciting and expanding for me to meet all of the people in the area. So accustomed was I to my solitude, and now there were people to talk with, a semblance of civilization...at least for a few hours a day. I so enjoyed the work (which was definitely for a left-brained person, not one who was accustomed to using her right brain) and meeting the challenges of a fast-paced setting, although on a very small scale. My new friend, Vangie, who had worked at the Post Office for over twenty years and became the post-mistress, recommended me for the position.

CERRILLOS, NEW MEXICO – JANUARY 12, 2003
OLD WINDMILL TRAIL

They came to visit me the second day at my new job in the Cerrillos Post Office...driving in a shiny white van all the way from Ohio on their journey to Tucson. I was not as prepared or stable as one would have hoped, because the day before my dog Nikky had to be put down.

Married since August, and yet we have not met. What will she look like? I caught a glimpse of Dad through the service window and opened the side door. "Can you leave to have lunch with us?" he said. "I can't, Dad, until the mail is up. Remember I told you this," nervously trying to make a good impression and continue on with my work. But the kind-hearted post-mistress overheard and said, "are they your parents? Go with them. I can finish this."

Life had dealt her some difficult cards, I was told. Orphaned at an early age, she was raised by two spinster aunts. Her husband of many years passed over in an automobile accident, along with the husband of one of her three children. She was riding in the car too. What will she be like?

Lunch at the Mine Shaft Tavern in Madrid is lost in my memory, yet afterwards, following me, they drove out the treacherous dirt road in their pristine white van to see my not-quite-finished and barely-furnished new house...surrounded by horses and cows, mountains and manure. Such a trooper she is. And not a hint of judgment.

We had tea at my tiny table, with a disgruntled Andy who was not expecting company, though it was not long and he was under her spell too. She brought a photo album containing pictures of their wedding and her family. She spoke of every single person with love and as her smile warmed the cold house, her heart lit the room. The name "Mary" suites her well. She walked among the animals without fear, as they were curious and intrigued by the new smells of the unknown humans. With five words, she won my heart. "It's beautiful out here, Karin," she said. My dad struck gold twice!

CERRILLOS, NEW MEXICO – 2003 AND BEYOND (Cont.)
OLD WINDMILL TRAIL

My job at the Post Office allowed us the currency to feed our twelve large animals. Shelters were required as well as fencing, and at one point we decided to form an animal sanctuary...The Olde Windmill Trail Farm Animal Sanctuary. Who would ever have thought this would occur? How grateful am I.

Following the formation of the sanctuary, another horse named Comanche, nicknamed Macho, came to us. I "saw" him in a dream before he made his entrance into my life. He had a small Arabian build, with a long flowing mane and a tail that brushed the ground. (You see, I had "asked" for such a horse which would expand our equine knowledge.) In our ignorance, we had no idea he would not immediately be accepted by the other horses. We did not know that (well it looked like this to us) they would try to kill him. He arrived in a bright red trailer attached to an enormous matching red truck, containing two disgruntled women, who were not only pissed off at the road they had endured but also could not wait to rid themselves of the gorgeous white gelding who could not be ridden. Poor Macho, who had been standing in a stall for years, was not prepared for what he was about to see...five horses roaming around in complete freedom.

As the women drove back down the driveway, Macho ran to the top of the Sacred Hill to watch. I could feel the sadness envelope his heart and attempted to comfort him until the horses, upon hearing the sound of the vehicle, appeared out of nowhere. There was not time for much of anything as the fighting and the whinnies and the chasing began. After several hours of this, we decided more time was required for his acceptance into our family of horses. Andy and I chased him into the enclosure which had been used for Nikky, and was still in use for our remaining chickens.

Within two days, we built a corral and a shelter and moved Macho into his new home, where he remained for almost a year...until God decided it was time for his release. You see, Andy forgot to close the gate one day and he was off and running free with the others. However, during that year he taught us much about caring for horses. Macho became best friends with the grey appaloosa Stallone and both delighted in pulling pranks on one another. He also became a "guard dog" of sorts...checking out every new visitor in their cars, before giving his approval and allowing them to open their door and enter into his domain. He kept this job for several years, until another horse, Cheyenne, took his place several years later.

Although my new job at the Post Office required much of my attention, I grieved for the loss of my Nikky so much that rather than wait until the grieving process had run its course, I rescued two puppies from an animal sanctuary in Glorieta, north of Santa Fe. I drove to the sanctuary one cold morning determined to come home with two puppies. The first one who touched my heart could be seen while walking towards the ten to fifteen puppies ready for adoption. He was black with white and tan markings and attempting to eat, while some older more aggressive puppies were shoving him away from the food. During the scuffle, this little one ended up with food all over his face. But Andy had asked for one with a "bull dog" appearance and I dismissed this little one for the moment, heading towards others who resembled bull dogs and sat down on the grass. Which one will come to me I thought as a beautiful tan female walked towards me and I picked her up into my arms. As one of her sisters followed suit, the director suggested it would be best to take a male instead. "Less fighting, you know. How about one of the black ones? They come from the same litter, different fathers of course," she said, and I searched for the little one with food on his face and picked him up too and fell head over heels in love with them. On the long drive home and amid much whimpering I "heard" him say his name was Zak, and his sister's name, Zoe. There is nothing in this world that heals a wounded heart better than puppies...and they worked their magic. The world became full of sunshine again. There would be more to come.

CERRILLOS, NEW MEXICO – MARCH 2003
OLD WINDMILL TRAIL

I am lying on the rocky and sandy soil, approximately two miles from my house and doing my best to avoid any cactus thorns...looking up to the dark, cloudy skies while communing with Mother Earth. I asked Her for him. The connection is felt and I leave, yet with some doubt. Did She hear me? Will She bring him to me?

My answer came two days later, when a neighbor a few miles away called. "I found the puppies. One of them survived. Do you want him?" The neighbor had been walking his dog and discovered the puppy, and although spotted by others he evaded rescue, not wishing to leave the body of his dead sister. Dropped off in this valley by an uncaring owner, they were attacked by the pack of wild dogs which ravaged the animals in the valley until they were all shot and killed a year later.

The neighbor took the puppy to a local vet who pronounced him to be within an hour of leaving this plane of existence. He came home to me covered in stitches and staples. "He will not be able to walk for several days" the vet said, "and may not ever be quite right." And yet he did not know my Rocky. (Such an appropriate name, don't you think?) The vet did not know what the soul within the tiny body, enormous head, and rat-like tail was capable of. We would soon find out. Rocky entered the house walking, and immediately made himself at home and acquainted himself with Zak and Zoe. His body healed and he grew and he grew, until the tiny body was in proportion with the head, and his partial Great Dane breeding became visible. And what a handsome dog he was. His mouth reaches the counter tops and his lethal tail wipes anything out of place, even negative energy. His brindle coloring, enormous size, and gentle nature attracts attention from all who see him, and yet the gentle giant takes it all in stride. He is my protector, so I have been told...another gift given, because I asked. Remember to ask. When it is asked from the heart, it is given. Always. There would be one more.

CERRILLOS, NEW MEXICO – JUNE 2003
OLD WINDMILL TRAIL

As they came in the door, Ann said, "they have your salt cedar, Karin," and I rushed outside the door to retrieve pieces of my newly planted tree from the mouths of three of my horses before it ended up in their stomachs, and put it back into the ground. "It will grow," she said, as I looked at her with doubt. It did...grow that is.

Sitting down with them to catch up on the conversation, Greg mentioned, "Rocky needs a friend." Why? He has two friends...Zak and Zoe. "They have each other. He has no one and he feels left out. He needs a girlfriend," was his reply. And so I "asked." And you now know what happened next.

A few weeks later while working at the Post Office, Sylvia, a customer, asked if I was the one with the animal sanctuary. "Will you take my dog? She's part coyote, you know."

She was of course the right age...six months, with beautiful golden fur and large brown eyes, and a tail that wagged so fiercely it almost rocked the back of the SUV which contained her. She came to me without hesitation as I asked Sylvia her name. She had none. So we drove off to her new life. Gracie and I. Her name is Gracie. And although Zoe, being the Alpha dog, was not fond of her, and many fights ensued, Rocky was smitten. She arises very early to roll on the ground, her feet kicking up high in the sky with gratitude for another day filled with fun and games... jumping up to take clothespins off of the line, or digging holes to hide within. She plays hard and sleeps soundly...a good match for the more serious and sensitive Rocky. (And me.) She follows me wherever I go, always curious and helpful. But this is not the end of Gracie's story.

By now you may be wondering what happened to the spiritual awakening? What happened to the talks with God, the meditations, the dreams? I seemed to have been focused on survival for so long that some of it went to the wayside...for awhile. Once living in the house, I continued to listen to the tapes from Gabriel and communed with my Creator, yet something changed. But you see, my consciousness had to expand to this point rather quickly to be able to love these large beings, these souls within the forms of fur and hooves and feathers, and for me to fulfill my contract (the animal sanctuary) made before entering this plane. It had been a part of the plan and it required much focus on my part, for I had changed dramatically over the past several years. Perhaps this period was a respite...a still point.

I had been painting, as you know, yet this time the subject matter consisted of the horses and the cows and birds surrounding me that I loved so much. My style of painting changed completely and the idea or "style" came to me in a dream. I was sitting next to a small pool of water, surrounded by people who were all watching as I placed my hand in the water and stirred it. Beautiful images appeared and this was repeated several times. Each time the image changed, the people present would ooh and ahh over that which they were seeing. This dream bled into the physical world as my acrylic paintings began to reflect and became not unlike the fluidity of water, and although there would be a realistic image in the foreground, the backgrounds were filled with forms of spirit. My paintings became a prayer of sorts. Yet the circle continues. It is never ending. There is much more to tell.

Chapter Eight

Many memories will flood into your system as you write as the observer.
You are not now as you were then. By expanding your consciousness
into Mine, you do see all sides of the spectrum and
you do reach higher and higher into the Divine purpose
of total enfoldment, always for the Greatest Good.
All is in Divine Order, no matter how you view it.
Simply put one foot in front of the other.

The sun sets quickly this cold winter's day, and darkness reigns for the moment as this side of Earth sleeps. And the angels shed their light upon all who ask. I choose the angels on this cold and stormy night to keep me warm. And as I remembered what he said to me, "sleep tight. Don't let the bedbugs bite," the writing began.

ZANESVILLE, OHIO – 1956 AND BEYOND

My father was a banker by trade, an athlete at heart. Positioned high within the ranks of the local bank, he began his quest at the age of sixteen. A George Mally he was...an honest soul. And all who received loans from him repaid, as he had earned their respect. He was tall and handsome and wore a hat and suit when we walked down the Main Street of my hometown. He held my hand as I looked up to talk to him. Everyone knew him. Everyone spoke to him. I was so proud of him, my Dad.

And when he returned home late after very important meetings, he would come to my room and tuck me in. With a kiss to my forehead he said, "sleep tight. Don't let the bedbugs bite." He loved and supported me throughout my childhood and beyond...me, a gentle, quiet child, and he, a strong, dynamic man. He taught me to ride a bicycle, to drive a car, to balance a checkbook, to always "do everything right the first time. That way you do not have to do it again."

And when I graduated from college, he was proud. And he "had a surprise for me," he said. "Meet me at the car dealership on Maysville Pike. I got something for you, Honey." And what a surprise it was! A completely restored Mustang, repainted in metallic gold, with black leather interior. And I thought to myself, "he really loves me." My Dad.

He and Mary continued their yearly visits and Dad came to love the land as I do. He enjoyed seeing the animals and walking within the serenity of the valley, and again was proud of his daughter who had formed this sanctuary for abandoned animals.

ATHENS, OHIO – 1974

"Oh Cath, it's no big deal. Just tell him the truth," I said loudly to her. "I can't Karin. I cannot do it. He is older than he looks, AND he is divorced, AND he has two kids. I didn't know all of this until they told me. Please just tell him I had a death in the family and had to go home."

My junior year at Ohio University in Athens, Ohio, living in a two room apartment with my best friend, Cathy, was interesting to say the least. Living within one bedroom, one 12 X 6 foot living room attached to a tiny kitchenette had almost destroyed our relationship. Two artists sharing such small quarters was almost impossible, but the rent was cheap. She was a potter and stacks of bowls and plates and cups adorned every nook and cranny. And the Taurus bull, meaning me, accidentally broke many of her beautiful pieces, although she always forgave me. My easel, located in a tiny niche of the living room was tripped over constantly, as were the paintings stacked in the bedroom. We were both very good...artists that is, and were rated high at the top of our individual class.

It was Spring term, a Friday night and another night of painting for me. I finally gave into her begging and pleas and promised to lie for her just this once. She hid in the bedroom when he knocked on the door. And there he stood...tall, attractive, not quite handsome, but I found myself staring into the most beautiful brown eyes ever seen on any man. He said, "I'm here to take Cathy out." I told him the lie and he said, "why don't you come with me instead?" "No thank you" was my answer as I tried not to smile too much.

The following fall quarter we ran into each other at a bar and I told him the truth of the lie and why Cathy did not go out with him. (A year older than me, she had graduated last Spring) We laughed and talked and decided to see each other again and again and again... until it was my turn to graduate and leave the most beautiful campus in Ohio. Although I returned to my hometown for the summer, I would drive back to Athens, to his house in the country, to spend the weekend with him and his sons, Chris and Todd, every Friday night after finishing my job at the clothing store. (As an aside, during the drives to Athens, I experienced somewhat "psychic" visions, lasting but a few seconds as they flashed before my eyes. As I rounded a turn or went over a hill, the same vision appeared in front of me, before I actually saw an event take place. Once I saw an accident, another time there was a house on fire. Or at times it was a stray dog.)

Monday morning, I made the journey home to Zanesville in time to start work at 9:00 AM. At this time, and through my Father's connections as the president of the school board from my high school, a job was offered to me in a nearby school district. It was a poor school district, with little currency for funding art teachers, and my job would be to instruct classroom teachers to teach art to their students. How could I, a twenty-two year old, fresh out of college, teach experienced teachers? This I asked myself daily, until my Mother gave me a way out.

ZANESVILLE, OHIO – AUGUST 1975 AND BEYOND

"No, once again. I do not want the word "God" used in my ceremony, Reverend Imhausen." "But you wish to have a wedding in my church?" he asked again. "Yes I do. And I gave you an excerpt from Kahlil Gibran to read for the ceremony." He finally agreed to this and walked away shaking his head in silence. You see I disliked attending church as a child and did not totally believe what they taught me. Unfortunately, in my ignorance, I equated God with religion. How wrong was I?

The summer moved by quickly. My mother, fearful I was being taken advantage of by Rich, (his name by the way), strongly suggested I stop living in two places, Athens and Zanesville, and either end the relationship or get married. Taking the low road on this decision was an easy excuse not to attain the job teaching art to the teachers, which terrified me. My ultimatum to Rich was either he marry me or I would move on. He chose marriage, and I found myself planning a wedding rather than preparing for my new employment. (And I must tell you that I loved him, Rich that is, but also he was a "father figure" of sorts, ten years my senior, which was fascinating to me.) My mother was recovering from a total hysterectomy and I was, for the most part, left with the wedding preparations alone.

It was a beautiful ceremony and tears filled many eyes. The two boys looked so handsome in their tuxedos as they took the vows along with us. Reverend Imhausen, ignoring my request, said the word "God" more times than I could count. My heart filled with sadness as we left the reception and my family and friends, to find a hotel before leaving the next morning for our honeymoon in the Poconos. They had horseback riding at the resort. Something to look forward to.

Within a week I found myself living in the familiar house in the country, located deep in Athens County, learning to cook from my mother's cookbook, and caring for the two boys. I also learned to say over and over again to the parents of the boy's friends and their teachers, "no, I am not his sister. I am his stepmother," as they stared until the statement sunk in. I became very busy as the only substitute art teacher in the county schools, and traveled almost daily to teach. Some days it was the high school and at times the elementary schools. And although I was completely in love with my husband and enjoyed the Friday nights we went dancing, homesickness set in. (It was during this time I had an out-of-body experience, a dream of sorts. One in which I "flew" over the downtown area of Zanesville, over the rooftops of buildings with a birds-eye view. I flew over the movie theatres, smelling the popcorn from the snack stand, and have not ever or since experienced such a sense of freedom and delight.)

Within a year we moved to Westerville, a suburb of Columbus, Ohio, where Rich became the manager of the Columbus branch of a large computer company. Finding employment as a layout/paste-up artist at a graphic design company in Westerville was quite enjoyable to me. The boys loved their school and became involved in baseball and karate. I continued my cleaning and cooking and driving the boys to their after-school activities. Rich often worked late hours and usually did not return home until dinner was over.

For Christmas one year, I bought the boys a Siberian husky whom we named Nikky. (Sound familiar? It was. His soul would come into my life again in a similar form and live with two more children...Ryan and Somer.)

My life began to become more exciting and fun, actually. On Valentine's Day, Rich surprised me with a red MGB and I sold the gold Mustang. I made some interesting friends at my new job. One of the artists considered himself to be a warlock and gave me some books to read which forever changed my life. I learned about life beyond the third-dimensional existence. Another friend, Virginia, introduced me to belly dancing. And what fun was that? Every Thursday night, I left my job to drive into Columbus with my leotards and cymbals to shake my body and learn the art of belly dancing, while Rich returned home early to care for the boys. I simply adored my teacher, Lois, who was so tiny and petite and graceful. As we became friends, I was introduced to Habeeba, the owner of the school. And for a while I was content. Yet something was amiss. Something was not quite right within my little world.

It came to be known that Habeeba's boyfriend worked for Rich and we began to get together socially...going to restaurants for quiet dinners, she and I chatting on the phone at night. And then IT happened. Habeeba called me in tears one evening and we met and talked. It was the night I took back my power. She said they were not working such long hours, Rich and her boyfriend. They were not slaves to their jobs as we were told. She became suspicious and followed them for several days. They left work before five o'clock she said, quite often, and went to bars after work. She discovered them dancing with other women. And with that my life with Rich ended. His attempt at an explanation was futile. However I waited almost eight months until another job came to me...a high-paying job as a graphic designer at Roach Inc. (During that period, no longer was I his slave. No longer did I do all of the housework and all of the cooking.) And at the age of 25, I left him, returning home to Zanesville in my little red MGB, with Nikky at my side. Driving back and forth from Zanesville to Columbus every day became quite tiring and I found an apartment near my new employment within six weeks.

And when the judge said, "are you certain you do not want half of the equity in the house? Are you certain he will only make payments on the car as long as you do not live with anyone else? Well in all my years as a judge, I've not heard anything like this arrangement." He looked down at me from way up high as I nodded my head in agreement. (Out of the corner of my eye, I could see Rich holding his breath.) You see, I could not take the house away from Chris and Todd. It was a horrible ordeal for them to experience. And I left feeling free, and without guilt, yet with very little assets. I began again. It would not, as you know, be my only divorce. A few months later the boys' mother Adda Mae passed away, and losing their house, their home, would have been too much for them.

CERRILLOS, NEW MEXICO – 2005 AND BEYOND
OLD WINDMILL TRAIL

Through my employment at the Post Office, new friends came into my life, however Saturdays continued to be spent with Marilyn and Ann enjoying our friendship at the beer picnics. We would go to each other's houses or meet at the local bar in Cerrillos, called Mary's Bar. We had lively conversations with Mary, the 92-year-old woman who owned and operated the bar with humor and a firm upper hand. All locals respected and honored her authority. Tourists enjoyed her wisdom and humor and went out of their way during their vacations in New Mexico to pay Mary a visit.

During this period I worked at the Post Office, spent time with the animals, painted, had art shows at various restaurants or wherever possible. I also met Somer for lunch in Santa Fe, or Ryan in Albuquerque, and visited Mom in Corrales, (where she moved after the sale of her house on Goldmine Road.)

Andy continued the ghillie suit business until there were no more orders. He built a round pen for the cattle to eat in peace, away from the horses, and a barn for shelter and hay storage. Soon there would be one more structure for him to build.

Well, you guessed it...we began to grow away from or distant with one another. I did not nor have ever enjoyed taking orders from anyone... especially from my husband, who had been a Marine Sergeant. And once again had given my power to another. This was the role Andy was playing as my soul mate. This is what we contracted for prior to coming to Earth. I had to learn not to give my power away. However living with an artist is not easy, and I thoroughly enjoyed my time alone painting and became resentful of his interruptions and the loud war movies he insisted upon watching and the fact that he did not work a real job like me. He also suffered from Post Traumatic Stress from his tour of duty during the war in Viet Nam as you may remember, and at times would suffer deep depressions and anger. I became unsympathetic and uncaring, tired of the constant battles, tired of the lack of communication. Following much soul searching, asked him for a divorce and moved into one of the spare bedrooms.

(As an aside, several years later, during a small group session with the one who channeled Metatron, it was mentioned that to judge, or dwell upon something that another person had created in their life, could also happen to you. Years ago while living in Clear Lake, the babysitter of my children mentioned to me that she was getting divorced for the third time. And I remembered thinking to myself, "how could anybody get divorced three times? How could anyone make three mistakes?" And look at that which happened to me.)

The first night spent alone in my bed was quite uplifting, and freeing as well. (And this may sound strange to you, but that night I felt a loving energy emanating from one of my paintings hanging above the bed.) The next year, spent living in the same house until the divorce was final and his new house was built near the barn, was not as bad as you may think. I simply did my thing, and he did too, and we remained partners in the caring of the animals and the sanctuary. You see, we had always been very good friends as well as husband and wife.

CERRILLOS, NEW MEXICO – JULY 4, 2006
OLD WINDMILL TRAIL

The date of July 4th could not have been more fitting.

"You said you would move out today, Andy. Today is the day." "I wanted to have it completely finished before I moved the dogs and Annie in, Karin," he said. "No," I exploded. "No!" A decision was made to split our dog family in half...especially since Zoe and Gracie did not get along. He would take Zoe and Zak to live with him in his newly built house a few hundred yards from mine. They were brother and sister. Rocky and Gracie would remain with me. Annie was his cat before the marriage and although I wished for her to stay with me, she went with Andy. It was truly a painful day...in more ways than one.

I did not listen to my intuition this day, for had I known what was about to transpire, I would have waited until he was ready.

It was time. He moved Annie first and returned for Zak and Zoe, putting their leashes on and preparing to walk out the door. I was holding Rocky and Gracie by their collars, and as he opened the door, Rocky lunged and Andy kicked him into me, which knocked me down to the floor, falling on my wrist. He was gone...and my wrist was limp and hanging.

I cried at the loss of him. I cried at the pain of my wrist. In agony I dialed his number. "You what? You broke your wrist? Call Ann...I can't go anywhere now," he said. Several minutes passed and he came back to take me to the ER in Santa Fe, only to return several hours later. They did x-rays, gave me a sling and pronounced my wrist to be broken in five places, but I would have to make an appointment with an orthopedic surgeon the following day. They would do nothing else.

Two days later Andy drove me once again to Santa Fe and I came home to my house wearing a cast from my armpit to the tips of my fingers. You may need surgery, they said. It will never heal properly, they told me. Six weeks later I would prove them wrong.

I was alone. I could not open a can of dog food. I could not feed the animals. I could not paint. I could not work at the Post Office until the cast was removed. I could not drive my car. But Ann came the next day bringing me potato soup and sympathy. Andy helped me when he could...and I slept and I rested and watched daytime television. Several days later, a woman, whose name I do not remember, paid us a visit. She was interested in our property and the animals, and was looking for a place to begin a spiritual retreat or sanctuary of her own. I told her not to come, but she did anyway, and I was forced to get out of my bed. Andy was taken in by her charm, her charisma, her interest in helping humanity and using our land and animals in order to do this...for free, I might add. This time my intuition did not betray me and she was ushered down the road and out of our lives. (I heard from a friend later on, she had approached several other property owners in the area with the same idea.)

A month passed by and with my large cast replaced by a smaller one, I looked for work...applying at the large galleries of Santa Fe on Canyon Road. Now divorced, I required more currency to support myself and Gracie and Rocky. But nothing came to me and I returned to the Post Office with gusto, choosing to somehow make my way. I took another job at a gallery in Madrid to assist with the currency issue.

CERRILLOS, NEW MEXICO – DECEMBER 2005
OLD WINDMILL TRAIL

A strange phenomena occurred early in the winter of 2005, a few days after Christmas. Leaving early for work one morning, snow began to gently descend upon the valley, and the further I drove the more intense became the snow. Speaking to God while driving was my usual custom, but as the snowfall increased so did the intensity of my prayers until I came to a steep hill and was forced to make a decision. There had been no forewarning as to the amount or voracity of snow this storm would produce and if I continued on this path, I may have become stranded and forced to walk home, my Jeep blocking the road. With that thought, I backed the Jeep down the hill and was able to turn it around. But just before I began my descent down, the sun peeked out for a few seconds, smiling and saying this was the correct choice. Driving home became more treacherous as the snow became deeper and deeper. When my Jeep came to a neighbor's house, whose property was adjacent to ours, I took a short cut through their property until I could drive no more...the snow was too deep...and walked half a mile to my house.

The snow continued its path of cleansing for another day, inch upon inch, until complete stillness. There was three to four feet, with drifts up to six feet. This part of Santa Fe county became the stillness as well. All were homebound. All businesses closed...including the Post Office.

Thankfully Andy had hay delivered the day prior to the storm and there was hay for all with the exception of Scarlet...the oldest cow, the grandmother of the herd. She made a decision to be alone due to a leg injury and was out in the valley without hay. I worried for her. I prayed for her, and sent energy to her. We searched as best we could. She was lost in the storm, presumed near death.

And then the phone calls began...neighbors asking neighbors if they were safe. And the questions began. "What can we do to remove the snow from the road?" "How can we get out of here to work and to shop for food?" Our road, Rogersville Road, although named by the county, was not owned by the county, or maintained by the county. What to do?

Andy called Greg, who, as you remember, ran the Cerrillos Gravel Yard and had access to heavy equipment, including a large front end loader. Greg agreed to do the snow removal and could be paid after the fact by everyone who lived out this way. It took him seven days to get to us. Another day to complete the entire project. He became everyone's hero as he would stop at each house at the end of every driveway to make certain all was in order. No one, including himself, knew how he did this enormous feat, as the road was not visible due to the depth of the snow, and the many dips and curves and steep hills. And yet he did. He was our hero.

Eleven days following the first day of snow, we were outside feeding when I spotted Scarlet walking very slowly up the driveway! She had lost a great deal of weight, but was alive. Truly a miracle we thought, running towards her with carrots and all the hay she could eat. I could see in her big brown eyes how proud of herself she was.

Chapter Nine

Stay in your place of peace as you write.
Be joyful, and love every moment.
There is no greater force within this segment of
Creation more powerful than love.

ZANESVILLE, OHIO – JANUARY 9, 1972
ASH MEADOWS

"Where is everybody going?" I said while getting out of my car after returning from a class at the local branch of Ohio University. It was a bitterly cold and a typical January day in Ohio, and they were all backing out of the driveway. "It's Ga-Ga. The hospital just called, Karin. Leave as soon as you can," Mom said to me and rolled the window back up. But as I was walking to the entrance of the hospital, they were walking out of it. "Honey, it's too late. She's gone," Mom said with tears in her eyes. My grandmother, known to me as Ga-Ga, had passed over due to a heart attack at the age of seventy-three.

Sadly I drove home and immediately went out for a run. Around and around the frozen lake in back of our house I ran until my brother, Ken, found me and suggested I come inside. And with sad high school boy eyes he told me it was too cold to be running and it was too dark. The following week was a blur. So intense was my sorrow, my grief, my guilt for not having spent more time with her. Barely nineteen years old, my sadness kept her spirit nearby. You see, an empathic person like me can, at times, feel those without form, ones who have passed over the veil. She came to me in dreams. She sat on my bed attempting to comfort me, and still I would not release her. This was not the first time something like this had occurred. After many months, I saw her for the last time in a "dream." She was enveloped in light, youthful again, her form moving upward to the stars and the heavens. And the communication ended.

ZANESVILLE, OHIO – 1953 AND BEYOND
BAILEY STREET

She had beautiful blue eyes, framed by dark glasses, and light grey hair. Her clothes were of the finest in town, in order to look her best when attending church on Sundays. She taught me to plant rose bushes and to sit very still and allow wild birds to come. They would light upon her lap or arm as she spoke to them. Her smile was constant for she delighted in even the smallest happening. Her house, although situated in one of the poorest neighborhoods, was painted frequently and "kept up." And she swept the porch daily, the sidewalk as well...the windows were spotless to allow more sunlight in for her beloved plants.

Living next door in a two-story white stone house were two women... a mother and a daughter. Their porch faced Ga-Ga's porch, and growing on their side yard was the most enormous weeping willow tree ever seen by me. I loved that tree. (Two hybrid willows were planted and continue to grow on two sides of my house at this moment.) Across the street and living in a ramshackle, unkempt house were an unmarried elderly couple. The man was black American, and the woman Caucasian. Although this would not be unusual today, it was at that time. Ga-Ga spoke in low tones when she told me of them, however there was no difference in her manner when she conversed with either of them.

The neighbors on the left side of her house were simply known as "The Weimers." Living within the untidy and dirty white shingled house were a husband and wife and their three children...their appearance as untidy as their house. There was a small pen filled with five or six hunting dogs in their back yard, for whom I felt great sympathy. They were only let out of the pen when the man took them hunting. Ga-Ga threw them scraps of food from her table as they were thin and hungry and barely kept alive, and I tried hard not to look at them. The sight of them made my heart hurt.

My brother and I spent Friday or Saturday night with Ga-Ga, so my young parents could enjoy some time with their friends. Mom would take us to her house in the afternoon and after she left we walked down the broken old sidewalk to the local market, the "L and B," to shop for our dinner. Our choice. It usually consisted of fried pork chops, homemade noodles, and canned corn. And, when in season, with fruit from the cherry or apple tree in her back yard, a pie would be made. Or if not, the most delicious popsicles were purchased.

As she cooked, I watched and learned while my brother, using a hammer, killed the ants on her sidewalk, and she so appreciated him doing this task. After dinner she gave me scarves to dance along with Lawrence Welk as she chatted with friends on the phone. We were always on our best behavior, for there could be nothing less in her presence. Every other weekend, one of us would get to sleep in her bedroom filled with red geraniums and sparkling jewelry.

Many years have gone by since her passing, yet the memories remain, and my brother and mother and I speak of her at times. It has been mentioned by psychics she has not returned to Earth, so needed is she on the other side. And along with her many other duties, she is a guide to my mother, my daughter, and myself.

CERRILLOS, NEW MEXICO – 2006 - 2007
OLD WINDMILL TRAIL

My mother, who was living in the tiny village of Corrales, near Albuquerque, became involved with a woman, a very gifted psychic, who channeled the high angel Metatron. As tapes of the sessions began to arrive, I listened while painting. At first the voice was inaudible, but with time I could "hear" clearly. The new knowledge challenged all learning acquired to this point, and seemed at times in disharmony with me, yet I could not stop listening. I had a few readings with the psychic, the one who channeled Him, until finally a reading with Metatron himself. And once again...otherworldly experiences entered into my sphere of existence. I learned of twin flames, and that we each have one in spirit on the other side of the veil. I was told that I am a child of nature. One lifetime was spent within the Elf and Fairy kingdom...the realm of Avalon, and I played a role during the time of King Arthur as a teacher. It was the last rising of civilization until this one...the last attempt to raise in consciousness the Divine Feminine. Another lifetime was lived as an Essene, during the life of Jesus, and my soul played another character, or so I was told. It was much to take in. From my understanding, all of us are playing roles, as if upon a great stage...helping each other to learn and expand our consciousness. No one is "higher" than another and there is no right or wrong. All are equal.

During one of my private readings with Metatron, he informed me that an angel was about to become "one" with me. This angel was an aspect of my twin flame. And this I will describe as best as I possibly can. Please listen with an open heart. I could feel myself becoming more at peace, and much more calm. I could sleep longer... there were no worries about anything. No cares. I cared not about who was doing what, or who was doing who. Nothing seemed to make me angry or upset, or feel guilt or envy. And I tell you it was absolutely wonderful. I began expressing myself without fear. I could feel the love surrounding me, emanating from within this angelic being. His name was given to me, but will not be made known in my writing.

Changes were occurring in my life as I was about to embark on a new job. Also, my daughter Somer was planning to relocate to Denver. My two part-time jobs, one at the Cerrillos Post Office, the other at a gallery in Madrid, as well as my art sales, were not providing me with adequate income. Following months of searching for employment, my friend Marilyn heard of a job opening at a business in Santa Fe. She worked as an insurance salesperson and sold a policy to this business. "The men are really nice," she said. I applied for and received the job because of my friendship with Marilyn, but also because they read what was written on my animal sanctuary website. The position entailed taking items from customers, researching these items for value, describing them and placing them on eBay for auction. (I worked with all men, except for one woman who came in periodically to box and mail the items) It was perfect. I was surrounded by beautiful things and the men were great to work for...and the three and a half days of work allowed me time to spend with the animals and to paint.

I left the two jobs in Madrid a few days early, before the new job was to begin, to see my daughter before she left. It was painful to believe she would be moving so far away, and Colorado seemed like another country. Somer and I drove to Tesuque to have lunch at her favorite restaurant, that made the best grilled cheese sandwiches, before she left for Denver with her boyfriend.

Ryan, after spending a year in Spain studying Spanish, graduated from the University of New Mexico with a major in language. While in Spain, he met a woman from Germany and they traveled back and forth across continents and oceans to spend a few precious weeks with each other. He learned to speak four languages fluently. He truly has a rare gift, my Indigo son.

My life moved very smoothly through the hot summer months, with great calm and poise, as this "one," this "angel" remained with me. The paintings came more quickly and easier to me, and began to "sparkle." I sold my art at local art markets and met some new artist friends, Caro and Eileen, who remain close friends to this day. (Caro was the first person to purchase a painting from me.) I made another friend, Mary, at a benefit for school children where my paintings were sold. All was going very well until Somer expressed signs of discontent with her boyfriend and her life, and she moved from Denver to Kansas City to stay with her father, Larry.

His intent was to get her back into college, for she had attended but two years in Santa Fe at the Community College, and he wished for her to graduate. He would pay for everything.

CERRILLOS, NEW MEXICO – SEPTEMBER 2006
OLD WINDMILL TRAIL

"What is going on, Larry? What is wrong?" I asked him during one of his frequent phone calls during Somer's stay with him. "I don't know, Karin, but she sleeps all the time. She doesn't do anything," he told me. He was terribly concerned, and in time so was I. Of course the conversations with Somer were quite a different story. But the gist of it all was they were not getting along, living under the same roof. Somer had been independent and living on her own far too long. This unease between them would cause a great rift in their relationship, which lasted for several years. While listening to both of them, a change stirred within me and I became involved again, involved with the drama of third dimension. It is difficult to explain, but my consciousness had risen above the third dimension for many months. I had remained a part of it, but not involved. And now the drama returned, and I liked it. Perhaps it was meant to be... perhaps not.

Eventually Somer called me and asked to come home. She did not wish to return to college and I knew something was very wrong, but not certain as to what it was...yet. A week prior to her arrival, a vision came to me. I saw a flash of golden light searing through my house which was to occur the day she was due to arrive. While I was at work, Andy came over to clean the batteries in the battery shed. As he opened the door to come back into my house he heard a huge sound inside. Whatever it was, and we do not know to this day, it fried the television set in my bedroom, as well as the one in the spare bedroom. Perhaps it had something to do with the solar power used to generate electricity in my house? But I think not. My child of the Golden Light was about to arrive.

I knew the moment she walked through the door, although it would be another day until she told me. She was pregnant and she desired an abortion as she no longer loved the father and could not bear to have his child. As I write this, the memory floods back into my consciousness. (Selfishly and secretly, I wished for a grand-child and had to put my feelings aside.) Arrangements were made, and I must admit my strength and support was not there for her as much as it should have been, so concerned was I that she might one day regret her decision. However, this was not to be. As a mother, I was also worried for her to have this procedure. This was her decision and her decision had to be honored...and she was right in her decision.

Several months later, during a reading with Metatron, I asked about Somer and the abortion. He told me the child was not meant to walk upon the Earth plane. That it was her twin flame who wished to be with her, to feel her, even for only a brief time. She and the father had lived many lifetimes together and they met to work through and balance a past Karma. (There is that Karma again peeking into another's life. I have decided myself to not honor any more agreements made due to Karma, but to forgive myself and anyone else for any "misdeed." It is all about intent and it stops this lifetime.) Somer believed this explanation to be true.

Chapter Ten

That which brings joy into your life, brings joy to Me...
for we are one.
If you forget everything else I say, remember this.

MADRID, NEW MEXICO – DECEMBER 2007

We are standing on the porch of the Mine Shaft Tavern, my friends and I, which include Ann and Greg, Marilyn and Mary, awaiting the start of the annual Christmas parade. It marks the beginning of the Christmas season in Madrid. On this day all of the lights will be turned on and many will drive to this small village to shop and enjoy the festivities. Wonderful smells of food cooking drift out to the porch and mingle with the smoke of burning cigarettes. People and their animals, including horses, llamas, dogs, and a yak, walk below us, dressed in their best Christmas finery as the parade begins.

Madrid was once a coal mining town and owned by the "company," complete with shops which contained all the necessities of life, before mining regulations turned it into a ghost town. Hippies moved in next and staked their claim. Those renegades of the establishment are now quite "established" and responsible artists and shop owners. Most are between the ages of fifty and seventy.

Many have joined us as we drink a beer in celebration of this day. Greg saunters toward me and stops for a brief conversation, which turns to his relationship with Ann. His 6 foot 5 inch frame leans down to me, his blue eyes twinkling and he speaks of his love for Ann and how grateful he is to have her at his side. There had been many opportunities to be with others, however, he said, "I know a good thing when I see one. I never strayed. Just want you to know that." Something is amiss I thought as he sauntered off again to speak with another. Why would he say that to me?

Joining my friends again, the conversation has turned to what one wishes to have done with their body when death arrives, although I wasn't present to hear the "after death" part. Ann was speaking...a woman with a heart of gold, the first to offer assistance to another, and one who always spoke her truth. She was describing a dream she had of being placed upon a high tier made of wood and lighting her body on fire, as some native American tribes did. Since the first part of the conversation was not heard by me and sounded as if she was speaking in the present I said, "but Ann you have much time, much life left." And she laughed and explained. Something was definitely amiss.

CERRILLOS, NEW MEXICO – DECEMBER 28, 2007

It was Friday morning and I was enjoying Christmas vacation away from my job. The normally sunny New Mexican skies were grey and gloomy. My phone was singing and it was Andy calling me from his house. "Come on we have to go. Vangie just called me. She heard a rumor in Cerrillos. Ann and Greg's trailer is on fire." I threw on some clean clothes and ran outside to jump into his pick-up. I called Vangie while riding out the dirt road, and she was not certain if the rumor was true, but would meet us at their property, located high in the Cerrillos Hills. "Fire trucks were spotted driving towards their property," she said. "That is all I know." It could not possibly be true. Could it?

It was. As Andy and I opened the doors to the truck and jumped outside Teresa came running to me sobbing, "they're gone, Karin. They're gone." (Teresa, a long time friend of Ann and Greg, was living in a trailer situated a short distance away, and had awakened to the smell of smoke. She immediately alerted the local fire department.) We hugged each other until Vangie arrived and joined us in disbelief. Although nothing remained but ashes where their trailer had once been, fire trucks and emergency vehicles surrounded the area making certain the fire was out, as Ann and Greg owned horses and chickens and emus. The enormous barn, the huge garage recently built by Greg, the equipment and gravel yard were all untouched by the fire. People from the media were filming the site and interviewing Andy. Marilyn arrived and our sobbing began again, until a sheriff began asking questions so he could identify the remains of the bodies. Marilyn became as professional as possible under the circumstances, and with the help of her years of insurance training, spoke to the sheriff with clarity.

We stayed and talked through disbelief asking each other how this could have transpired, and finally drove back to Cerrillos...to Mary's Bar, to check on Mary, who, well into her 90's, was another friend of

Ann and Greg. We all secretly hoped she knew. She did. We found her sobbing at the loss of her friends. Marilyn used Mary's phone to call Ann's daughters in Phoenix...not an easy task to do, but Marilyn has great strength. Ann and Greg had driven home from visiting her daughters just the day before.

That night, while drifting off to sleep and thinking about the day, I felt Greg's presence. The feeling received was, "all was as it was meant to be...not to worry." They were fine.

Ann's daughters arrived the following day and Marilyn and I walked with them on the land as they stared in disbelief and shock at the tragedy. Her son would arrive a few days later. As weeks passed it was discovered their furnace was the cause of the fire. They left for Phoenix a few days prior to Christmas and turned the thermostat down to conserve on propane, and upon returning home, turned it up again. There was a default in the wiring, which ignited. The toxic fumes caused their death while they were sleeping. They felt nothing. Such a relief to all of us.

A wake was held at the Mine Shaft that following Friday. Those whose lives had been touched by one or the other attended. Never have there been so many at the bar. Ever. I had no idea of the numerous friends they accumulated over the years.

Several months later on a cold March day, Marilyn and I drove to Ann's favorite spot on their property. It was a tiny shack built by some friends, with a sign that read "Cash Entry." Located upon the top of a mesa, the views were incredible, especially with snow patches visible on the north side of the hills. Together with the brisk March wind assisting us, we scattered the ashes of their remains to the north, south, east, and west sides of "Cash Entry." And when the task was completed, two bluebirds appeared. We looked at each other with amazement. And we knew. The birds seemed to be watching us. Bluebirds were Ann's favorite birds, and seen only in flocks, not as a pair. Ann and Greg were visiting with us.

Several years later, Ann came to me in a dream. Within the dream I saw myself traveling in a boat on a strong current of water, following a river which led to a small village. The homes were constructed of stone and wood, some in colors of red, and were located high on the banks overlooking the river. Yet my boat took me past the village to the outskirts, to a place where Ann lived, somewhere in time, somewhere in heaven. As I opened the door of her house she was busy working with many people surrounding her, watching her. Greg was barely visible and off to the side. But what I remembered vividly from the "dream" was the smile on Ann's face. She had found peace. She was happy. (Through this experience came the understanding that there is little difference between "us," who dwell in the physical, and those who have passed through the veil...to the "other side." They are simply without form.)

Chapter Eleven

And with the illusion of birth,
came the illusion of death.

CERRILLOS, NEW MEXICO – JANUARY 2008
OLD WINDMILL TRAIL

"Stephanie has been staying away from the rest of the herd lately and I have been walking out to feed her," Andy mentioned one cold January day after the morning feeding was completed. It was Saturday and I was home. "She has been standing out that way," he said, pointing to the south direction of our property. I decided to look for her and left immediately.

The night before left a sprinkling of snow which sparkled like diamonds and made crunching sounds under my feet. The sky was clear. The winter storm over. Crunch, crunch, crunch. Her form appeared to be still... no movement at all, and I picked up the pace. Closer still, another form became visible and I began to run. It was a calf struggling to stand for the first time...a beautiful white calf with spots of golden brown. She made it up to all four legs. Two coyotes were smiling and watching the scene, waiting to make their move. When they saw me and heard my scolding, they ran off, but not far.

"What is your name little one?" In silence I heard "Sara" something. "We will call you Sarafina." Stephanie was very weak and very young... too young to become a mother, but I remembered the wild bull who had made his presence known last summer. Telepathically I told her she must move her baby back to the barn to safety, away from the coyotes. With the last strength she could muster, the three of us began the slow, arduous mile back to the barn, stopping occasionally for Sarafina to nurse. When home, we brought food and water to the exhausted mother.

It takes great courage to become a mother in any species...great courage. Stephanie continues to groom her daughter, her only child to this day, although Sarafina is fully mature...an adventuresome cow who walks without fear. A few months after her birth, Michael, a bull-calf deep brown in color, with a white spot in the shape of a half moon on his forehead, was born to Ariel. The two grew up together and became best friends, although their mothers are arch enemies. Sarafina is the smallest of the cows, while Michael the largest in size, making quite the odd couple. Both of them acquired the skill of jumping fences and must be rescued occasionally from being trapped within a neighbor's property. They are also unafraid of the horses and at times eat with them, a great privilege I might add. You see, horses feel themselves to be superior to the cows and chase them with delight and purpose.

CERRILLOS, NEW MEXICO – APRIL 2008
OLD WINDMILL TRAIL

His mother brought him to us as a young calf, ill and thin. A viral infection the vet informed us, possibly heart problems. And so began the years of giving him antibiotics whenever the coughing began. Carrots seem to soothe his raspy throat. He loved the attention of two adults worrying and fussing over him, our Gabriel. He became so very tame and expected the same treatment from all humans who came for a visit. And of course they did as he expected.

Several months ago, the coughing began and the antibiotics did not work this time. Other remedies made of herbs were given to him, but nothing helped the raspy cough. The vet decided he must have at some point in his life swallowed some wire and that we must tie string around a magnet and drop it into his mouth and pull out the wire. There seemed to be no other solution, yet we could not do it. We were not cowboys and Gabriel weighed over a thousand pounds. Even if we were able to do the procedure, we were afraid the magnet might become lodged within his body, and so we did nothing as there was nothing to do but pray. I placed him on a healing and prayer list and he was the first animal to appear upon it. All of the healers informed me they gave him all they had. We truly expected a miracle. But after several months, Gabriel went out on his own...away from the herd. For weeks we searched for him daily and brought food and water. It had been over a week now, and we could not find him.

One warm April morning, while washing my dishes, I heard a

tremendous sound and it came closer and closer. The cows had been down at the pond drinking water from the stock tanks, and as I ran outside the entire herd was running in a southerly direction past my house. Ravens were flying overhead high in the cloudless sky...coyotes following closely behind. There was a gentle breeze blowing in from the south. I grabbed my cell phone and ran out to follow them, calling Andy. He quickly caught up to me. The cows were lost in sight, but a few coyotes returned to take us to the spot of his diseased body. And there he was...our beloved Gabriel had made his transition near the spot where Sarafina was born a few months earlier. We discussed the burial and sadly walked home with the grieving cows who had lost a family member. They did not graze that day, so upset were they and simply laid outside of the barn in great sadness, in stillness.

Although completely aware of the Grand Illusion in this third dimension... that being there is no birth, no death, only the illusion of one coming into form and the illusion of one leaving, did not help me at all. I knew he was eternal, but asked Metatron in a private session several months later about his passing. He told me it "simply was his time" and "he will meet you at the Gate." It was no help either. I missed him and he was gone...my Gabriel.

Chapter Twelve

*What a true gift this life has been...to feel, to touch,
to taste and smell, to see and express love
from within a physical form.*

SANTA FE, NEW MEXICO – AUGUST 2008

It was a gorgeous August morning...still and peaceful, not a cloud in the Santa Fe sky. My car was parked a short distance away as I walked towards my office. A stranger, a woman appearing to be in her mid-thirties, was getting out of her car. She looked at me and said hello. "You look familiar. Don't I know you?," she asked. Walking a few steps towards her, my eyes took in the perfection of her form, the beauty of her appearance...very stylish, European perhaps, and mentioned something about how familiar she appeared to me as well. "I used to work at the Cerrillos Post Office. Many know me from there," I told her. "Well, I do not know Cerrillos, but I do know you. My name is Anna." We shook hands as I told her my name and stared into her eyes which were covered with dark sunglasses. She smiled and said it was good to meet me. Continuing to walk the minute it required to open the door to my office, I turned around to look back. She and her vehicle had disappeared. Something extraordinary had transpired. But what?

Several months later, an answer was given to me from Metatron, during a session with the woman who channeled Him. "Remember when I told all of you that some of you might meet an angel? Well, you met one." "She said her name was Anna." "You know her. You know her very well. She was your cousin during the time Yeshua walked," he said. "Well who was I?" asking in a shaky voice, remembering that I recently finished a book titled "Anna, the Grandmother of Jesus," written by Claire Heartstrong. "You were her cousin Elizabeth" he said. "I remember the name and I will look her up," fighting my voice to not ask who she was. As I write this, I do not know whether it to be true and will not elaborate on this.

SANTA FE, NEW MEXICO – SEPTEMBER 2008

I could feel tension at my place of employment. The owner was simply agitated and not himself. I spoke with Nancy, a fellow employee, who, as you may remember, boxed up the items to be mailed. We were now good friends and shared similar beliefs. Something doesn't feel right, I told her, and the sales are so low. Sleeping was difficult, which for me signals a change. Yet it occurred only on the nights before I worked, which were now but three days a week. I actually did not know how I could continue working with such little sleep. The other days were enchanting and I was happy painting and spending time with the animals. One morning a week later, when awaking from sleep a voice told me "You will receive a gift from God this day." That day at work, they laid all of us off. And another beginning began.

ALBUQUERQUE, NEW MEXICO – DECEMBER 2008
THE MATRIX GALLERY

"You guys, I cannot have a beer with you. I have to work tonight." My friends Mary and Marilyn decided to drive me to my first opening on a Friday night at my new gallery in Albuquerque. It was such a sweet thing to do. We stopped in Cedar Crest at Molly's Bar for a drink on the way. "I have to speak with prospective customers" and preferred to do it without alcohol on my breath. But this did not in any way deter them and after a quick beer, and a diet coke for me, we were on our way again.

It was one of the best galleries in Albuquerque, located on Central Avenue (the old Route 66) within the up and coming Nob Hill area. I knew the area well as Ryan lived there since college. Contacting the owner via email, produced an interview and a viewing of my paintings. And she accepted my work! Before leaving, the owner, who was quite pretty, young and stylish, told me she had seen my work several months earlier when I had a show in Santa Fe at a local restaurant. She also told me she was a Wicca, and felt at ease relaying this information to me. Why do people tell me these things, I thought, smiling while walking out of the gallery. Why?

We stayed for the required two hours...me schmoozing with potential customers, Mary and Marilyn flitting about, having fun, enjoying the Opening. Mary, a Texan beauty, with blue eyes and bright blonde hair, pretended to be interested in one of my paintings, drawing attention to it. Ryan came as well and seemed to enjoy himself.

Ryan has always been my strongest support, and encourages me and my art in any way possible. We began the drive home to Madrid. I had sold nothing...but it was the first night and my expectations were high. My friends believed in me too...so blessed am I with such good friends as Mary and Marilyn.

The following twelve months were filled with job searching and painting, when not doing the sanctuary chores. In the spring I joined a group of artists who displayed and sold their work every Saturday morning next to the Farmers Market of Santa Fe, and did quite well. It seemed no one was interested in hiring a 55-year-old woman, and none of my paintings sold at the Matrix gallery, so after six months I removed them and focused on the market alone. In the summer I joined the Corrales Society of Artists and once a month on Sundays, drove to the tiny village situated near the Rio Grande River and sold my art on the green grass-covered park. The two markets were more than enough work for me, yet the job searching continued.

CERRILLOS, NEW MEXICO – FEBRUARY 2009
OLD WINDMILL TRAIL

Oh no. Oh dear God no! Not my son. I was awake the rest of the night, waiting before calling...part denial, part sheer terror.

He had appeared in my dream at the age of about two years, wearing a diaper and swimming in a pool of water. Not happy was he, my son. As I watched him swim, the pool became filled with dark red blood. What has happened to him?

After several days, maybe a week, I called. But there was no answer. I worried and waited until the next day when my phone sang its song and heard him say "Mom, I've had an accident." And as I was so grateful he was alive, I could calmly say "What happened, Honey?" Through muttered tones, he said, "we were walking home and it was late and dark and I fell down some stairs and into a pole...not really sure. But my face, Mom. It's all cut up." "Where are you?" I asked. "At John's apartment" (His best friend from high school.) "I'll be there in a few hours." And we arranged a time and place to meet.

I mentally prepared myself while driving the scenic Turquoise Trail to Albuquerque, taking the back roads to Central Avenue, to his house in Nob Hill. He was not there yet, but within a few worrisome minutes his friend John drove up and Ryan emerged from the car. And I saw him. My tall, striking, handsome son, had stitches covering a cut on his face from the corner of his right eye down to the right corner of his mouth. "You look much better than I expected Honey," I said, as we both cried and hugged. We drove home to the valley of the healing spirits, surrounded by the animals of fur and feathers and hooves.

And he slept and slept as the land and the angels worked overtime for him. I placed him on a healing list, and although at the time there was no faith in this for him, he would soon see the miracles which were about to occur.

I called a nurse friend who recommended the best plastic surgeon in Santa Fe. Miraculously we got an appointment the following day. And I do mean this was a miracle. There had been a cancellation. We drove to Santa Fe for the appointment in silence. When the nurse called his name I remained in the waiting room, unable to go in with him. But when he returned there was a crooked smile upon his face. Plastic surgery would not be necessary and in time most of the scar would completely heal. It appeared to the doctor that a plastic surgeon did the stitching. They did not charge us for the consultation. Another miracle.

Several days later I drove Ryan back to Albuquerque, to the hospital to have his stitches removed. "Oh Mom," he said, "we will be here for hours," he said while viewing the waiting room filled with people. I smiled as his name was called and we left within twenty minutes. I reminded him of the healing list. Another smile appeared on his face. "There were many praying for you." I drove him to his house in Nob Hill and returned to my sanctuary in the valley.

We all have what is known as wake-up calls. (One of these wake-up calls would come to me in the future.) His face did heal in time, all but for a very small section. One that could not be overlooked or forgotten or ignored. It seems most of us have preferred to learn the hard way, and the faster way. If it were not so we would not have come to Earth.

ALBUQUERQUE, NEW MEXICO – JULY 2009
PARADISE HILLS

"Mom, what do you want done next?" I asked while taping a box.
"Why don't you start on the art supplies, Karin. They won't be so difficult," she said.

My mother was leaving New Mexico. Several years ago she sold her condo in Corrales and purchased a house. It was a beautiful white adobe, built upon a hill, deep in a neighborhood of Albuquerque known as Paradise Hills. There was a great view of the mountain from her patio, and she could watch the giant balloons during the Balloon Fiesta in October. Her taxes had greatly increased and, as she said, "I'm not getting any younger." It was time to go home, back to Zanesville, where my brother and his family lived. The house sold, the papers were signed, the movers were coming in a few days, and her flight was booked. I was quite sad at her departure and would miss her terribly, but tried not to show it. This was the last week and I was helping her pack.

The final day came, and the movers were here. We watched as they carefully placed all of her belongings in the huge truck. She would stay with my brother in Zanesville until she found another house. I drove her to a hotel near the airport as her flight left early in the morning. As I left the motel to drive home to the valley, I felt so alone. Somer was gone...and now my mother.

Chapter Thirteen

You may find yourself being drawn to the past.
And again, observe and allow all to flow through you
as if drops of rain were falling upon your face,
as if angels' wings were touching your heart.

CERRILLOS, NEW MEXICO – NOVEMBER 2009
OLD WINDMILL TRAIL

The number of animals which Andy and I cared for at the sanctuary remained stable since the births of Sarafina and Michael. Snowy, Star, Co-Co, Ci-Ci, Stallone, and Machi made up our equine family. Our herd of cows included Scarlet, Rosie, Rafina, Miguelly, Paint, Tiffany, Stephanie, Cory, Uriel, Joshua, Ariel, Michael and Sarafina. We thought our number of animals would remain the same as we denied any requests of taking more. It was all we could handle. But this was not to be, and one by one they began to arrive.

The summer months were filled with tension as many of our neighbors, and when I say neighbors, this includes anyone living within a six mile radius, began releasing their horses out to graze. The released horses came to visit quite often, creating chaos among our horses...some of which were territorial. Snowy was by far at the top of this list. And much kicking and fighting and biting and whinnying ensued.

In November Cheyenne came to us after escaping from his corral, neglected and hungry. A tall paint was he. Strong and beautiful he was. He had left her many times over the years, only to have her take him back, tied to the back of her Volkswagen, walking the four miles home. This time she, his "owner," did not come for him and he was content.

We assumed by the time cold weather arrived to the valley, that the owners of the released horses would take them home. We were incorrect.

One December evening, as the snow fell and the wind blew, utter chaos broke loose as all of the released horses descended upon us at once...and it was feeding time. They were all very hungry, their eyes filled with fear. What could we do? We could not turn them away...so we fed them. And they stayed. Contacting the owners was of no use. Many simply were no longer living in the valley, due to the economy and unable to keep their homes, let alone feed their horses.

The following week, we named the five horses and one donkey. The tall, young, buckskin mare we called Maya. A small but sweet Tiger

Mustang was named Luna...her golden brown daughter, Tessie. Ellie was the name chosen for a beautiful young paint, and her very young daughter was named Arianna. Arianna had developed a horrible habit of eating manure, and it took many months to break her of this. A tall roan gelding, who was and still remains a disturber of the peace to put it mildly, we named Ranger. Last, but not least, was the tiny donkey. We called her Miss Stella. We now had 13 horses, 13 cows, and one donkey to feed and care for. We became a bit overwhelmed. Once again, we assumed this would be the end. There would be no more. Once again, we were incorrect. (And I must say here, we absolutely loved each and every one of the newly-arrived horses and enjoyed having them with us.)

CERRILLOS, NEW MEXICO – SPRING 2010
OLD WINDMILL TRAIL

In the early spring of 2010, two horses began to appear when we were feeding. Only, this time we knew their owner quite well. He adopted the two the previous year. One was a beautiful black Draft who was named Velvet. The other horse, a shy and tiny black mare we named Lily. They both won our hearts. Velvet was rescued from standing within a ten by ten foot stall, and Lily had been to auction five times. Our neighbor told us that due to his new baby, he could not afford their upkeep and was looking for homes for them. We decided to take them in, fearful of what might happen. And believe it or not, Velvet became "best friends" with the little donkey Miss Stella, and also her protector.

Late in the Spring, another horse arrived at our expanding sanctuary. We had no idea of where she came from and asked everyone we knew. Tired and frightened this little dapple grey mare was, and we gave her a home and named her Blossom. She became what I call the "cheerleader" of the group of horses...small and tiny, yet cheerful and a friend to all. She is quite popular with visitors and many say she looks like a "fairytale" horse.

I continued to sell my art at the Art Market on Saturdays in Santa Fe, but noticed my sales were not what they had been the previous year. My unemployment had run out, and life was becoming quite difficult. I discontinued my monthly sojourns to Corrales once a month, as my sales were not equaling my effort and the rising cost of gas. It was hard work, loading up my jeep with the huge tent and tables and paintings, setting up and tearing down, and considered a change. It was time.

The change came in October. A neighbor, Sharon, asked to come out to my house for a visit. She lived at the beginning of the road, near the highway and had not been out as far as I live. She simply loved my paintings. She happened to be friends with the owner of a well established co-op gallery in Madrid. Sharon said she would contact her friend and see if she could arrange an appointment with her. I actually thought nothing would come of it. It did.

I met with Liz, a tall blond in her mid-seventies who could pass for a sixty year old and the owner of Spirit in Art Gallery. The following week, I brought several of my paintings and prints to the gallery, and to my amazement, there was an available space and she loved my work. A few days later, several of the other artists within the co-op also approved my work. It would be several weeks before I was able to get everything ready to hang and sell. And another beginning began.

Chapter Fourteen

Smell the roses as you move through this existence.
Take a moment for fun.

CERRILLOS, NEW MEXICO – OCTOBER 2010
OLD WINDMILL TRAIL

Why must it all happen at once, I thought while frantically throwing clothes into my suitcase? And now they want to see the animals the day after I return, plus the fact that all of my paintings must be ready a few days later. Two generous women, Nancy and Bonnie, decided to assist us in generating money for the animals and wished to see them when I returned. And this morning another absolutely gorgeous horse showed up while opening my door to walk outside and feed Snowy. He was a tall roan gelding with a blonde mane and tail, well cared for complete with his shoes attached, but with the now familiar frightened look in his eyes. While feeding him I began to ask his name. He seemed quite content to stay near Snowy and my door, so I placed an inquiry on the local email. The result of which was a neighbor calling with the information that she spotted an unknown white truck hauling a horse trailer out the road, heading in our direction the previous night. He was intentionally dropped off! Something did not feel right about this, but there was no time to dwell upon it as the phone sang. Nancy and Bonnie ordered some hay for us and a truck was on the way, but someone had to meet it at the end of the road.

Spirit. We will call him Spirit.

COLUMBUS, OHIO – OCTOBER 2010

It has been such a long time...almost twelve years.

Her breath smelled of the tomato juice she was drinking...mine of a light beer. The four-hour layover at Chicago O'Hare was over and we were about to make our descent through the cloudy skies towards our destination... Columbus, Ohio. She was in her mid-seventies and spoke with a German accent, and we began conversing, my seat mate and I. We spoke of many subjects such as her concern with her daughter-in-law, my concern about feeding my numerous animals.

"Do you know many people who had root canals over twenty years ago now have to have the tooth removed? The dentists did not get out all of the infection, you know." Well that was a strange comment to make. "And you should check out my website. I can get your supplements cheaper, you know," she mentioned in her German accent. "Castor oil is very good for wrinkles," she informed me. We talked and talked and the flight seemed but a few minutes and she was gone. The plane landed. (A year later I had to have a tooth extracted, due to an ineffective root canal completed over twenty years ago. She was, unfortunately, also correct about the castor oil.)

Dad and Mary met me at the gate with a hug, but Dad appeared worried. "A woman just told us you were on your way, Karin. She was very nice. German I think," Mary said, as we walked towards the luggage area. But it could not be found, my luggage, as I searched and searched. Finally while filling out the forms for its retrieval, it appeared as if by magic. My dad was so upset about it all, but Mary whispered that it was good we were delayed. "Your dad was worried about driving through the Columbus rush hour."

As we seated ourselves in the white pristine van, the arguing commenced over directions and speed. And secretly I was grateful for the beer on the plane and watched the flat landscape of Columbus become the familiar rolling hills...almost home...almost home.

ZANESVILLE, OHIO – OCTOBER 2010

We did not drive to Mary's house as expected, but stopped on the way to see some old family friends...the Zeeks, Jennie and Roy. Their daughter, Vicki, my best friend through grade school and college, was present too. (Later that summer I would be so very grateful we stopped for that visit.) The previous year Vicki survived ovarian cancer and did not look well as palsy had appeared on one side of her face. Yet we talked as if I had not been away so many years, so much time. "You have to meet Jake my grandson, Karin, before you go," she said, and I was thinking how can I possibly fit it in.

Jennie reminded me of an incident, which I did not then nor ever have any memory of, in which I beat up her son Scott as a child. She watched us from a window of her house, and although surprised and shocked at my actions, cheered me on...even against her own son. "You were always so quiet, Karin," she said, noticing a change in my demeanor since the last time we met. "So shy."

Weariness began to set in as I had awakened at 4:00 AM that morning so we decided to leave Jennie and Roy and Vicki. My 77-year-old father was now on familiar territory and the speeding increased as we flew over hills and valleys, eased through stop signs, raced through red lights. In record time we made it to Mary's house. As we got out of the van I swore silently that he would not be the one to drive me back to the airport.

Although it was almost dark, the familiar Ohio landscape remained visible, and their house was surrounded by blue spruce trees, located near the river, on the south side of town. Mary's house, although beautifully and tastefully decorated, was somewhat suffocating to me. Heavy curtains and drapes were hung over the numerous windows. Yet when I saw a room she called "The Porch," the uneasiness disappeared. The windows were free of fabric and there were Halloween decorations everywhere. The room in the distant past had been a patio for her family and was eventually closed in to make additional space. It held a huge picnic table and rustic furniture, and we sat down to eat some homemade cookies and milk before going to bed.

I awoke early with but few hours of sleep, due to the excitement of the day and the barking of a neighbor's dog. I showered and dressed and walked outside early to see the lovely Ohio landscape on a crisp October morning. Fog settled in near the tall trees and I breathed in the moisture, which had become so unfamiliar to me.

Dad and I took a walk after breakfast and spotted deer in the woods nearby. After lunch we drove around Zanesville seeing the sights and remarking on all of the changes which had occurred in the last several years. It was time to take me to Mom's condo, on the North side of town, and we sped through the familiar yet changed streets of my hometown.

Full of light and crystals, my mother's condo contrasted greatly with Mary's house. Her latest metaphysical paintings adorned every wall. We all had dinner after my brother and his wife arrived. Ken, filled with his usual joviality, had many stories and jokes to share. And I must say my 50-year-old sister-in-law never looked better. She always seemed to me to be the reincarnated spirit of Snow White. With her porcelain white skin, coal black hair, rosy cheeks, and long black eyelashes which framed her bright blue eyes, she was quite striking. She had not aged a bit. It was so good to see them both. Due to my art market schedule, I was unable to stay the weekend and missed seeing my nephews who were away at college.

Later Ken drove me, and very quickly I might add, to see his new home...also situated within a wooded area. The house was large enough to hold two families and he was very proud of his new acquisition. It was three stories high and covered with brown thatched wood. At Christmas time, his favorite time of the year, the house would become a Christmas wonderland. And every room within his huge house had its own Christmas tree. Tiredness once again came to me, and we rapidly drove through the city streets...back to Mom's condo in the woods.

I fell asleep on her sofa and was awakened by her tiny cat, Newton, who was licking my face, informing me it was time to go to bed. In the morning Mom reminded me to take a long shower...a luxury I had not enjoyed in some time. I lived in a desert after all.

"I cannot believe she didn't come, Mom," I said while dialing her number in Columbus. There was no answer. "I hope nothing is wrong." Mom, distracted, acted as if she were not surprised. Why am I always surrounded by psychic people? My friend Karen was supposed to come for brunch this morning, and since she didn't make it, we prepared to drive to the cemetery to see my grandmother's grave. You might be thinking this would prove to be a solemn occasion. You might be wrong.

The skies were blue and filled with the familiar puffs of white clouds. The cemetery dazzled with trees of red and gold, pink and orange. Quietly we searched until her grave was located. We bowed our heads for a few brief moments until I turned to look at the nearby lake. "Oh look, Mom. The doves are swimming on the lake!" And with that she began laughing and said, "they aren't doves, Karin. They're swans." We both began to laugh, and the laughter turned into hysterics. As we doubled over in laughter and tears filled our eyes, a car with many staring passengers drove by slowly. Undoubtedly the passengers were feeling sad to see us in such "grief," which of course made us laugh all the more. (I'm quite certain many Earthbound souls, upon hearing us, made their departure that day.)

As we staggered to her Subaru, Mom said, "let's go to lunch." We were going to The Muddy Miser which was located by the Muskingum River near the "downtown" area, next to the old Mould Shop. This restaurant served the best onion rings in town, and I'd been drooling over them for years. By this time you might be thinking the rest of the day would go by smoothly. You might be wrong.

My mother recently moved to Zanesville and was having difficulty navigating us to the restaurant, as she rarely came to this part of town. At least she drove at a normal speed. As we were driving under a traffic light on Sixth Street, I saw something white out of the corner of my left eye heading towards us. Suddenly we stopped abruptly and she yelled something and placed her arm over my chest as if I were still a young child. "Oh my God, Karin. Did you see that?" The "something white" was a huge truck and it had just gone "through" us. It did not hit us, but by some miracle, ended up on the other side of us. The driver apparently not seeing the red light, or us. "Did you see that, Karin? Did you see that white truck go through us?" she said as we drove to the restaurant. This type of extraordinary event had occurred to Mom before and although visibly shaken, (as was I) she was grateful to have a witness this time. The only solution found by us was that our angels were working overtime that day.

We arrived at the restaurant around noon and not a soul was in the entire place. Strange, very strange...especially because of the location near the downtown area which was filled with bank buildings and government and attorney offices. The restaurant was decorated with Zane Grey memorabilia. Zane Grey happened to be my grandmother's favorite author and throughout her lifetime she had devoured every one of his books.

"You can sit wherever you like," a very cute and pregnant waitress informed us. And over a very hot steaming plate of the best fried onion rings ever made and a cold beer, we discussed the events of the day and spoke with the waitress. After lunch, as we walked to the Subaru, I looked at the old Mould Building. My Uncle Jody, Mom's brother, worked there for many years. I had worked in the same building...but at the time it was no longer the Mould Shop.

ZANESVILLE, OHIO – OCTOBER 1995

I was working in the old Mould Shop on the top floor. 5 B's, the company I work for, had leased it for their warehouse, their Human Resource department, my office with Julie, and the executive meeting room.

Recently promoted, I began working in this space with Julie, who was ten years my junior, married into the family-owned company to the man who happened to be the president. She was embarking on a new adventure...one in which I became a part of. They were going to open stores with their own embroidery on t-shirts and sweatshirts. And guess who would be creating the new designs? Me. It was due to my writing that letter several months ago, standing up for myself... voicing my opinion.

ZANESVILLE, OHIO – AUGUST 1995

"But he did not tell them, Jeff," I exclaimed loudly to my friend and co-worker. "He did not tell them. I heard them talking." The Production Art department was located in a vacant doctor's office on the east side of town, and each of the artists had their own "examination room" so to speak. It was great. Mine even had a bathroom attached to it, and it was next to my supervisor's office. Recently promoted to Creative Artist, most of my time was spent creating sketches for prospective customers. Although I loved the job, I became increasingly dissatisfied while watching my designs embroidered on garments and dwelling way too much on the amount of money being made, and also the fact that none of it seemed to come my way. And then an incident happened. All of the artists were asked to create designs for a very important customer. And we did. I overheard the conversation between my supervisor, whose office was adjacent to mine, and the president of the company asking who created the spectacular ones... and as he described them, I knew they were mine. But my supervisor claimed he had no idea which one of us created them (and perhaps he did not know) and said it could have been himself. And I sat fuming in the room next door...hearing all of it. My ego was hurt.

A week later, at the suggestion of my friend Carol, who was a department manager at 5 B's, I composed a letter expressing my concerns and hurt feelings about the conversation which I'd overheard and sent it to one of the family members...thinking I would be fired within days. A few days later one of the sisters of the family walked into my little office and said my letter had been read in front of the entire family at their Sunday dinner. Oh my God...what was I thinking. Yet instead of being fired I was promoted, and with a raise this time, by Julie, and relocated to another office building. It had been a great learning experience for me and I became a tiger in the business world, working hard to acquire more money to support my children. And for once, standing up for myself had paid off.

ZANESVILLE, OHIO – OCTOBER 2010

Mom and I had an uneventful drive back to her condo and she retired to her computer room, and me to my phone calls. My friend Karen called to tell me she got the weeks mixed up and thought we were to meet the following week. It was so good to hear her voice. We had written or emailed over the years, but not talked with each other on the phone for quite awhile. Vicki called to insist that we meet for lunch the next day so I could meet her grandson Jake, and I was to return to Dad's house and meet some old friends from 5 B's later on.

The next day, we met the Zeeks, Vicki, Jennie and Roy, and the sweetest little two-year-old boy, Jake, for lunch. He was truly a joy and most definitely an Indigo child, so bright, so full of love. All of the waitresses at the local Bob Evans knew him. Vicki decided to visit me in New Mexico next summer for a visit. We made some plans.

After lunch we drove back to Mary's house to wait for my dear friend Jeff, an artist from 5 B's, who would pick me up and drive me to see his ex-wife Carol and their daughter Leah. Jeff informed me through email, that he had become hard of hearing. This will be interesting. It was my last night in Zanesville and I would return to Mom's condo. Not wishing to put my father through anymore stress, Denise, my sister-in-law, agreed to take me to the airport the next morning.

When Jeff arrived I said my goodbyes and we climbed into his pick-up. He seemed much taller, much larger, than I remembered from twelve years ago. Due to his loss of hearing, he yelled unknowingly to communicate with others. For some reason, he was able to read Dad's lips and they understood each other. And with hugs to Dad and Mary, we left the house by the river and the blue spruce trees.

"I REALLY LIKED YOUR DAD. HE'S A COOL DUDE," Jeff said loudly as we drove at record speeds over hills and valleys to God knows where. "YOU LOOK JUST THE SAME JEFF." We yelled at each other the entire drive in order to communicate, with me clutching the door. I have no idea of how much he understood me...but he was the same old Jeff, and it was so very good to see him. We finally arrived at our destination. Carol's house. A serene and peaceful Carol met me at the door.

Leah, their daughter and their pride and joy, was re-introduced to me, and she was a beauty. I had not seen her since she was four years old. We sat and talked for a few hours until it was time for Jeff to drive me back to Mom's condo...again at record speeds. What is it with these people?

Jeff stayed briefly to admire Mom's paintings and left. I watched him walk to his truck, wondering how he really feels. You see, Jeff had been a talented singer who wrote music and played the guitar. Several years ago he made a CD of himself singing and playing a guitar to all of the songs he wrote. His soul must have known that deafness would envelope him, and he listened.

The next morning Denise and her sister Lona, a ray of sunshine, drove me to the airport and by five o'clock in the afternoon I was home within the valley, surrounded by horses and cows, mountains and manure. And the dream continued. When will I wake up? When will the dream end? When will I see the truth of it all?

Chapter Fifteen

My love and your love combined, sends the power of love to all.
As you combine your will with My Highest Intention,
everything around you changes for the greatest good...
it is the highest power of the universe.

CERRILLOS, NEW MEXICO – MAY 2011
OLD WINDMILL TRAIL

Springtime produced little graze in our valley and we were forced to feed our horses and cows well into the month of June. In recent years they grazed and we fed but once a day, along with treats and carrots. But this year the high desert became barren and dry and no spring wildflowers appeared. Some of the neighbors were doing rain dances to the spirits in hope of calling the desired spring rainfalls into the valley. As Mother Earth was shedding her skin and moving higher, we had to learn to adjust to Her changes. And with the assistance of others, we did.

Nancy and Bonnie visited our sanctuary the day after my return from Zanesville. As promised, they offered their support. Bonnie painted a beautiful poster and Nancy printed several hundred of them. I placed them along with information about our work with the animals within stores and shops and restaurants throughout Madrid and Cerrillos, and the surrounding area. Most owners chose donation jars so they could simply ask their customers for donations and give them a poster. This worked very well for awhile and we received a little here and there. It helped with the rising cost of the hay.

Our greatest assistance came from a woman named Megan, whose sister was a friend of Nancy's. Megan was a writer for Care 2 Causes. She wrote about the humane treatment of animals and when she came to Santa Fe to visit with her sister, she decided to write an article about our animals and our sanctuary.

I met Megan at the end of the road, and she did not seem to mind traveling out the treacherous road and/or the long distance. She was also quite interested in our lifestyle...living off the grid. When we arrived she simply breathed in the beauty and serenity of our sanctuary. She loved meeting Snowy and at this time another horse, Co-Co was in the corral with him due to her severe hoof problems. (I don't know if it was the wild mustang in her, but she hated to have our ferrier work on her hooves, and had to be mildly sedated. And even at that, she fought him.) The article was well written and when it appeared on the huge website, donations began pouring in. She mentioned our lack of adoption policy and the fact that the animals are able to free range and that none are confined to corrals with the exception of Snowy and Co-Co. Our financial difficulties eased a bit due to the number of donations.

CERRILLOS, NEW MEXICO – EARLY JUNE 2011
OLD WINDMILL TRAIL

Cholla cactus cover the valley...quite tough and mean and prickly they are. But once a year they are not unlike the butterflies and bloom the most magnificent fuchsia blossoms. The entire valley resembles a giant rose garden. The blossoms bring bees and hummingbirds and eventually the flies, and the sounds of buzzing and humming fills the valley with the song of summer.

"Hey Vicki. How's it going?" "I don't know yet, but something is wrong...the doctors are doing tests, you know. I'll be fine and as soon as this is over I'll be out to see you," Vicki told me when I called her. My stepmother Mary mentioned in a phone conversation that Vicki was having some difficulty. She was sleeping a lot and tired easily. "You might want to give her a call Karin." I did.

CERRILLOS, NEW MEXICO – LATE JUNE 2011
OLD WINDMILL TRAIL

"She had a fall, Karin. She's been staying with Jennie and Roy. She's in the hospital. Here, I'll give you her number," Mary said when she called a few days later.

"Hi, Vick. How are you feeling?" "Oh, they are poking and prodding me, you know, but they still don't know what's wrong. God always takes care of me," she said with what I imagined to be a smile. " When I fell, my head could have hit the floor, but I landed on Dad's foot," she said in a voice that was barely recognizable. "I'll be out to see you when this stuff is over." We talked for a bit, but it was time to go. "You take care, Vicki. Love you."

A week later she was released from the hospital and had not been diagnosed with anything, only to return several days later and finally be diagnosed with Multiple Meyeloma cancer. Her daughter immediately had her moved to a cancer hospital in Columbus, Ohio.

CERRILLOS, NEW MEXICO – JULY 2, 2011
OLD WINDMILL TRAIL

"Hi, Honey. I've got some bad news for you. Vicki passed away last night," my dad said with sadness in his voice. There was nothing they could do. My heart stopped for a moment. My best friend was gone...at least from this plane of existence.

Her funeral was on Friday, but it was one I did not attend. A few days later, while sitting in my sunroom enjoying a quiet moment, her spirit came to me. She asked me to tell her mother and father, Jennie and Roy, that she was OK. "Tell Mom not to worry," I heard quite clearly. She stayed but a few moments and was gone. She had kept her promise. She visited me in New Mexico, but how was I to give her mother Jennie the message, since she was so very much into religion. The answer would come soon.

CERRILLOS, NEW MEXICO – EARLY MARCH 2013
OLD WINDMILL TRAIL

March was such an unpredictable month. Would there be snow? Would the wind and the rain come? Or would it all come at once?

Late in December, following the winter solstice, I awoke for three nights in a row to see 3:21 on my digital alarm clock. I knew the angels were informing me to have my book finished by March 21st...the very important equinox. My life must be released, my body cleansed. And yet I waited until the last moment and humbly asked the Creator of this universe for assistance, and continued with reviewing and writing about my life, while staying alone for three weeks...not seeing anyone. Remember to ask. Also, believe that which you ask will come to you.

CERRILLOS, NEW MEXICO – JULY/AUGUST 2011
OLD WINDMILL TRAIL

My art was selling very well at the gallery called "Spirit in Art." It was located in Madrid and keeping me quite busy. Along with selling my paintings, prints and cards, I began painting animals on flat rocks, which were mounted on wood and I named them "Petroglyphs." My days were filled with gathering rocks, sanding and staining the wood, and painting. Two days a month I worked at the gallery and it was so much fun to spend a day in Madrid, to talk with other artists and tourists. Life was good.

Following the morning chore of feeding one day in the heat of the summer, I retired to my studio to paint. Outside could be heard loud whinnying and the stomping of hooves. I ran outside. To my amazement the commotion was created by the entrance of a small white horse, who, to put quite simply, was skin and bones and barely able to walk. None of the horses who came to us were in such poor condition. Obviously, someone had corralled and neglected her, otherwise she would have been grazing. (Monsoon rains produced the greatly needed graze.) It was, after all, the middle of summer. Needless to say I did not ask around for her owner, because if one came looking for her, she would not be returned. Our young gelding, Ranger, who seemed more like a stallion than a gelding, decided to "claim" her for his own. He was charmed by her, and in doing so protected her from the other curious and rambunctious horses, keeping them away from her, allowing her time to heal...to gain her strength and weight back. We named her Violet, and although Ranger eventually lost interest in her, she was accepted by the other horses.

CERRILLOS, NEW MEXICO – AUGUST 2011
OLD WINDMILL TRAIL

My life changed little as summer came close to the end, except for one incident...a mystery which has never been solved.

One morning upon awakening, I looked to the right side of my bed to see a tall, rather ordinary looking man with black hair, wearing a rather ordinary white shirt and black pants, staring down at me. There was absolutely no emotion upon his face. Now what? And the vision faded. I dressed to go outside to my Snowy and Co-Co and the ravens and coyotes, in somewhat of a daze, thinking of the man.

Later, as I walked outside again to feed the rest of the animals, Andy came towards me saying rather excitedly, "Do you remember last night? Do you remember Karin? I had the most fantastic dream. I was with aliens on board a ship. You were there. We looked outside and could see the Earth from far away." "What did they look like? Ordinary?" I asked. His answer was yes, just like ordinary people. And I told him of the man, from an extraordinary world I had seen earlier that morning, and of all the visions I'd seen at night of ordinary looking people, none of whom were known to me. I do not know why they came, and Andy seemed believable. But it was not a dream. They meant us no harm. Perhaps they were simply observing us? Perhaps helping us? I do not know...however strange bruises appeared on my upper arms occasionally, before this occurrence.

CERRILLOS, NEW MEXICO – SEPTEMBER 2011
OLD WINDMILL TRAIL

September...my favorite time of the year. The snake weed and Apache plume are blooming and decorate the high desert landscape with spots of color. Sunflowers bloom along the highways of Santa Fe. There is a chill in the mornings followed by sunshine and warmth in the afternoons.

While sitting in my sunroom, thoughts of Vicki float through my consciousness as I watch Andy walking towards my house with something in his hand. He recently returned from the Post Office. It was an envelope from Vicki's mother, Jennie. There was a card inside with a brief note from Jennie. While cleaning out Vicki's house, her daughter Lyndsay, found a card with a post-it note attached which said "Karin." "She meant for you to have this, Karin." I could feel Vicki's presence as I looked at the birthday card with tears in my eyes. There were pictures of two little girls walking hand in hand, and the little girls looked very much as she and I looked many years ago. I left to feed the animals, but when I returned she was in my sunroom.

"Please, Karin, tell my family that I am doing well. Tell Mom not to worry. Tell them I am OK." Yet I still did not know how to do this.

The answer came in a dream that very night. In the dream I saw Vicki in a house...a brown wooden house. She was with her grandmother. The small house was filled with antiques. (Vicki collected antiques all of her life. She was quite an expert.) They seemed so happy. And I heard the now familiar words. "Tell my family I am OK. Tell Mom not to worry."

The next day I wrote a letter to Jennie, thanking her for sending the card, and described the dream of Vicki, and relayed her message. A few days later Jennie called to thank me for telling her of the dream. "I was so worried, Karin. I did not know where she was, and now I can visualize her with her grandmother in the little brown house." And I learned a very valuable lesson. The lesson was to simply be myself and to tell the truth. It may have saved Jennie much grief if I had done what Vicki asked in the first place, and is the reason for the writing of this book.

CERRILLOS, NEW MEXICO – DECEMBER 2011
GOLDMINE ROAD

"You want me to what? Give a speech? Oh, Barbara, I do not give speeches unless I prepare in advance." But she insisted, "you have to do this Karin. It is the appropriate thing to do. Don't worry. I'll get you started."

The party was quite elaborate. The house was enormous and decorated with Christmas cheer from floor to ceiling. There were well over a hundred people in attendance, which included almost all of my friends. Mary, Marilyn, Eileen, Caro, Teresa, Sharon and a dear neighbor, Bob, decided to attend this benefit/Christmas party including many neighbors whom I knew when I lived on Goldmine Road.

Several weeks earlier, Barbara contacted me asking if she could combine her annual Christmas party with a Benefit for our sanctuary. I immediately agreed. She also asked me to bring some paintings to sell. Huge posters were made with pictures and stories about all of the horses and cows. Barbara asked everyone who attended to bring a bale of hay, or purchase one from the local feed store. And they did. We received many cash donations as well, and many of my rock paintings were sold. My hair was cut and new clothes purchased for this event. Barbara and her husband Tom were both animal rights advocates, and Barbara was well known for all of her philanthropic work in this area. It was so very kind of them to do this for us.

Now it was close to the time for me to give a speech, I nervously searched for Marilyn to give me some encouragement but she was involved in deep conversation with a man. Barbara began speaking to the group of people and motioned towards me with a question. All I could remember was applause. Apparently I left my body and spirit took over, because everyone said it was a great speech, one in which is lost in memory to me! The party was a huge success.

I was invited to spend Christmas Day with Teresa and her family and friends. Marilyn was going too. Christmas morning I drove the familiar road past Cerrillos up the hill to the property once owned by Ann and Greg and made a left turn to Teresa's trailer nearby. Teresa decided to stay on the property following the fire, caring for all of the trees and flowers planted by Ann and Greg. It was a warm day for December and after our Christmas lunch we sat outside and talked. Hours later I drove home to make some phone calls and speak with my children.

Several days after Christmas, I went to the Cerrillos Clinic for a check-up. My blood pressure was extremely high. My doctor asked if something was wrong. Was I under stress of any kind? We recently had to put down the high-spirited wild mustang Co-Co. "Have you given yourself time to grieve? You must take the time to grieve," she said. And so I did. Yet later I would discover this was not the reason my blood pressure was so high.

Chapter Sixteen

It is but a second...a lifetime is. This you will come to know as your vibration increases, as your soul light intensifies, as you embrace the immenseness that is you... that is all of you.

CERRILLOS, NEW MEXICO – 2012
OLD WINDMILL TRAIL

The year 2012 was the long-awaited year for metaphysicians and those of spiritual teachings and religious backgrounds. It was to be the year our Great Mother Earth, our beloved planet, would ascend into the fifth dimension. And all those who inhabited Her body would ascend with Her...if they chose...if they graduated. I had such very high expectations. This year would be the best year yet, albeit knowing there would be many tests to pass before "graduation" into the higher dimensions, and in my naivety was completely unaware of the difficulty or the number there would be. Some tests were passed. Some were not, as you will soon see.

The year began so very well. Andy and I became friends with a woman named Bobbie, who lived at the beginning of the road. Bobbie was a 4'11" ex-army nurse, a Command Sergeant Major during the Viet Nam War. She is also an animal lover, and decided to financially assist our sanctuary, promote my art, and help Andy sell his books. And although I received a grant from the Equine Protection Fund of Santa Fe through a contact made at the benefit in December, the donations were not enough to cover the enormous cost of hay. Bobbie became an angel to us in many ways. She contacted a friend, who happened to be a grant writer...one who had not ever lost a grant. Her friend wrote this grant for us, combining Andy's efforts in assisting the troops suffering with Post Traumatic Stress, while employing some of our gentle horses and cows for healing, thus benefiting both non-profits. The grant would provide funds for the printing of Andy's books as well as hay, building supplies, and veterinary costs for all of the animals.

Several years ago Andy wrote a book entitled "A Warriors Guide to Insanity," describing his experiences in Viet Nam and his struggle with life afterwards, including his efforts in adjusting to a non-military lifestyle. The grant was to last for three years. You have no idea how excited we were at the prospect of this occurring. Until the grant was approved, Bobbie gave us her financial support. We would know if the grant was approved in April...or so we thought.

MADRID, NEW MEXICO – FEBRUARY 2012
HIGHWAY 14

"What do you think, Bob? Do you like this horse here?" "Oh, Karin, it's perfect," he said in his soft-spoken voice as I stepped down from the ledge, viewing my work.

My neighbor and friend, Bob, recently purchased a ramshackle old adobe house, located two miles south of Madrid. It had been abandoned for several years until vagrants and drug dealers occupied the space.

"The house needs a mural," he told me one day, stopping me on the road to talk. "I would like you to paint it for me, Karin."

Once a physicist, working at the Los Alamos Lab and now quite wealthy, he was thoroughly enjoying his retirement by restoring this old house...using found objects and treasures for his decor and also items that function in unusual ways. And although it was primitive, even by my standards, I simply loved his creation. His toilet was fashioned out of a huge bucket filled with peat moss with a toilet seat attached on top. When a shower was required, a valve was opened in the shower stall to allow water which was collected and solar heated on the roof, to flow by gravitational force down through a shower head. Quite ingenious, and much more efficient than having to use an outhouse. Located within the same room as the toilet and shower was a small indoor greenhouse, once again employing the sun's rays for growing the plants as well as heating the room.

The only other source of heat were two wood burners...one in the kitchen and one located in the living room. The wood burners heated his coffee in the morning while his food was cooking in a solar oven outside. His nod to "normal" conveniences were a huge sink with running water and a propane refrigerator. Donated or found partially used cans of paint were mixed to the desired color and painted upon the adobe walls, resulting in each wall being a different color. And to my artistic eye, the colors seem to flow and work well with each other. Bob did not own a television set, but instead listened to a radio and read books. We discussed a wide range of topics during my painting days, including the Native American culture, the Aboriginals of Australia, and the destruction of our beautiful planet...all the while uplifting Hispanic music emanated from his ancient radio.

Bob's front door was opened wide when the sun appeared on that side of the house, not only to invite in the sun, but also to allow a wild bird to fly inside and eat a piece of his homemade bread. It flew through the door when he whistled. (I might add here that Bob seemed impervious to either extreme cold or heat, once appearing at my house in the dead of winter wearing nothing on his upper torso but a long-sleeved shirt and a fleece vest held together with a piece of duct tape. The zipper was broken, as he cared not for appearance or vanity.) He is one who has learned to do the dance of life, has achieved the freedom of wealth, the respect for all, and is at one with himself and our Great Mother Earth. I thoroughly enjoyed my time painting the mural with Bob and his dog, Pepper, at the little adobe house surrounded by juniper woods.

MADRID, NEW MEXICO – FEBRUARY 2012
FIREHOUSE LANE

My gallery in Madrid, "Spirit in Art", closed its doors in January and re-located to a smaller gallery across the street. The six original co-op artists relocated too. I was not asked to go and must admit my feelings were a bit hurt, but a man named James arrived, leased the shop, and renamed it Treasure Box. I was asked to stay...myself and the remaining five artists. Although it was easier than looking for another gallery, something did not feel right and a premonition came to me, which was ignored. I say this to you...never ignore your feelings...they are more important than that which your brain tells you. As other artists were brought in to fill the empty spaces, what was once a gallery, became indeed a treasure box, filled with crafts, and although beautifully and tastefully executed, my so called "fine art" simply didn't fit in. And when asked to work at a small shop nearby one or two days a week, I gratefully accepted. After all, it was only temporary. Our grant would be approved in April.

CERRILLOS, NEW MEXICO – APRIL 2012
OLD WINDMILL TRAIL

The stillness brings a sense of calmness to this valley of magic, manure, and a sprinkling of junipers. While driving home from my mural job, I prayed. My sales at the gallery have been so low I had no idea of what to do, so I asked to acquire more currency. The last four hours were spent climbing up and down ladders at Bob's house and my body was tired and my mind weary. Yet upon arriving home, I checked my email to find one from my gallery. Many items sold and more were needed to replace the sold items. How can this happen so quickly?

I went outside to see my Snowy...to brush him, and the calmness returns. He is my man and though it sounds trite to say, many will comprehend this bonding of one form to another. He was standing within his shelter and I began brushing his tangled mane, his back, his legs... white fur settling on the ground. And softly I wished for a small wind to carry the fur away and out of his corral. At that moment a tiny dust devil appeared at the north end of his corral and came gently towards us, circling the shelter picking up Snowy's fur. It left his shelter, flew up over the fence, deposited the fur on the ground, and disappeared. I thanked the little dust devil. How much better can it get?

During this quiet moment, Andy came running towards Snowy's corral. "It's the grant! We received the grant!" And I believed another beginning was about to begin.

We expected the grant money to arrive within days, or weeks. When the grant writer called the corporation for which the grant was written, she was informed the currency would begin to be dispersed in August. It would be only four more months. We could wait.

MADRID, NEW MEXICO – MAY 2012
HEAVEN BOUTIQUE (OUTSIDE PATIO)

"Are you expecting a great deal of money coming to you?" she asked. "Yes," I replied smiling inside. "It is all over the cards you know. I also see that you are quite intuitive, empathic like me." "Why don't you listen? Why don't you do what they tell you?" she asked while peering at me through her dark glasses. "I do the best I can but am not always certain if what I hear is coming through my brain or spirit." "You need to listen to what you hear and follow through. And I don't like to say this, but I think you need therapy, or at least someone to talk to. Your friends don't even have a clue, you hide it so well. You are holding too much in, and it is necessary to release it, because when you go, you don't want to leave any part of you behind. Do you understand?" I again nodded in agreement. "I see many animals around you. They are your friends, aren't they?" "Yes. I am writing a book about my life and the animals." "You need to finish the book. It will assist in the releasing. This is very important during these times. You must also surround yourself with white light, every morning and every night before you go to bed. And be cautious when asking for angelic assistance. Most of them are ET's. You will know an angel when you see one. I saw one once and I will never forget it. You are also very concerned about your daughter. I will give you some ideas as to what to say to her, but I must tell you, she feels that nothing is wrong." And she did. "Our time is almost up. You should also use sage to cleanse the body every morning and night, and cedar to invite positive energies to you. It will help. Also use lavender oil as well."

It was my first tarot card reading and it was quite informative. She was good and I left with the determination to release the past.

CERRILLOS, NEW MEXICO – MAY 2012
OLD WINDMILL TRAIL

Two weeks have passed, the most two difficult weeks of my life, bar none...or so it seems. My answer was no, then yes, then no again... my final answer. I feel so much lighter. The decision has been made and painting will come easy to me this day, until the phone sings, and it is Andy. I answered with trepidation as the call is originating from the VA in Albuquerque and after his "hello" he handed the phone to Pete, his VA representative. Pete, once again pressed his point that I should remarry Andy, and reminds me that if he passes over all will be lost, the sanctuary, the animals, the homes, my life. "Andy may die while driving home today. Then what would you do? What would you be left with? Nothing. No VA benefits. No healthcare. No income, no animals, no nothing." Anger begins to fill every cell of my body, and my answer once again, was no.

Many thought me to be crazy for not remarrying Andy. He had been receiving extra money from his monthly VA disability check as they were under the assumption we were still married. A recent questionnaire was mailed to Andy asking him to declare his marital status. Although he informed the VA many years ago of our divorce, the additional benefits continued to come. But with that came a dilemma. Either we remarry, and when he passed over the benefits would go to me (having been married over 10 years in total) or Andy would have to pay the VA back the additional money he received over the years. His friend Pete worked for the VA for many years. The simple solution would be for us to remarry and divorce a year later. But it simply did not feel right to me. And this time I passed the test and listened to my feelings. Besides, was it not dishonorable? And believe me, I am well aware of the dishonesty and treachery of our government. But does it not have to stop somewhere? So my answer was no.

TAOS, NEW MEXICO – JUNE 2012
THE RIO GRANDE RIVER

"Pull her in! Pull her in by her life jacket! Now!" I was absolutely doing my best, but the raft was spinning and her life jacket was not tight around her body and came up over her shoulders when I pulled up on it. The guide was yelling at me from the back of the raft. Denise and I were seated at the front...or we were. Denise was now in the river.

The premonitions began over two days ago. They came to me as visions and I could see someone in the water and myself jumping in to save her. But I did not know who it was, and began to mentally prepare.

My friends, Denise, Mary, and Marilyn, decided a year ago to spend holidays and birthdays with each other. We were single, and not all of our children lived near us. And so it began. It was so much fun. On Mary's birthday in December we drove to Santa Fe to see a Revue, a comical play with singing and dancing...definitely executed Santa Fe style. For Marilyn's birthday we drove to Albuquerque to play Bingo at the Route 66 Bingo Hall, and for a drink at Molly's Bar in Cedar Crest afterwards. On my birthday in May, which happened to fall on Mother's Day, we had lunch at a Cuban restaurant. It was now Denise's birthday and we were to go white water rafting on the Rio Grande, an activity I'd always wished to experience. It was supposed to be a leisurely journey down the river, with little paddling or navigation involved...simply enjoying the river and the sunshine. And today was the day.

I had to put my premonitions aside. It was Denise's birthday wish... mine as well. The morning was overcast with a slight breeze and the further north we drove the colder the temperature became. Upon our arrival to meet our rafting company we were informed that we would be upgraded to a "higher level" known as "The Racetrack" and we signed the release and consent forms. Denise brought another friend Sandy to join us. We asked if we could all be in the same raft. Our wish was granted and we watched the safety instructions (I paid very close attention to these instructions) and put on our life jackets before boarding the raft. I must add here that we were all in our late fifties or early 60's and stuck out like "sore thumbs" as everyone else was much younger. We all decided that Denise could hear and follow instructions well and the guide placed her in the front left side of the raft. I have no idea why the guide placed me on the front right side. As we headed out into the river, we were told to listen to her instructions and follow either Denise or myself...depending upon which side of the raft one was sitting. Immediately we all knew we were in trouble.

It seemed like a dream which was orchestrated for us all...a nightmare of sorts as we crushed into rocks and spun around through the rapids, the young guide yelling and screaming at us. And then it happened. We ran into a huge rock and the raft tilted to the side filling it with water and Denise fell into the cold river. Since I was the closest one to her, it was my responsibility to pull her out. I handed her my paddle, but she was able to grab the side of the raft. I yanked on her life jacket but it came up over her head. Marilyn was pulling on the back of my life jacket with all of her strength to help with leverage as the raft spun round and round. Sadly, I could not lift her up. The guide was forced to come forward to the front of the raft and do it herself. Denise was a trooper and regained her composure and we proceeded on our course. All of us were exhausted and cold and there was yet another hour to go. Surely it would pass by smoothly. It did not.

As Marilyn and Mary began speaking to our guide in a calm voice to ease the situation, Sandy went overboard and none of us could pull her up either, except for the guide. When Sandy was back on the raft she didn't know where she was and Mary, a nurse by profession, began yelling "She's stroking. She's stroking" and that brought Sandy back to reality and we continued on our journey. And I must say there were no, and I mean no, peaceful moments until we were within sight of our landing when we all relaxed. Gratefully we opened our car doors, turned on the heat, and headed for Española for lunch, which included two margaritas apiece. We all told Denise that this experience by far exceeded any of our birthday celebrations to that point. She agreed.

CERRILLOS, NEW MEXICO – JUNE 2012
OLD WINDMILL TRAIL

While sitting in the sun room my eyes followed the white clouds drifting by within the bright blue New Mexican skies. When will it all happen? When will the Lady Geya make her transition? What will the new Earth look like? And I heard, "she will be illuminated with light for ALL to see. Patience. Patience."

CERRILLOS, NEW MEXICO – JULY 2012
OLD WINDMILL TRAIL

The skies are filled with flies of all sizes and shapes and their sound of buzzing fills the air, as the tails swish back and forth...the hooves go stomp, stomp, stomp...the bodies covered with mud. The monsoon rains have turned the hot, high desert into a mud hole, and the horses and cows become as children, rolling in mud to wipe the pesky insects from their bodies. My house is filled with not only the same irritating flies, but also a mice invasion. And this morning a young bull snake was discovered slithering through a spare bedroom, and immediately taken out. I have killed over fifty flies this day, not usually my style, as they are normally captured and taken outside. I realize that if you kill once, it's much easier to do the next time. Later I sat down to my computer and watched it crash in a futile attempt at downloading a program. I began to feel sorry for myself, sorry for the flies, sorry for my life, until I heard the words..."this too shall pass." They were the words of my grandmother, who, although she departed the Earth plane many years ago, was able to comfort me when nothing else would. This day was another test, I assumed, and it did not matter to me whether I passed or failed.

CERRILLOS, NEW MEXICO – AUGUST 2012
OLD WINDMILL TRAIL

August, the month Andy and I have been waiting for has finally arrived. There would be no more worries, no more stress. We were planning where to place shelters and what improvements to make for our animals. It was such an exciting time anticipating the future...and it was bright indeed.

The beginning of August brought not only high expectations but also another horse...a horse we had come to know very well over the years. His name was Cinnamon, and was owned by a neighbor who released her horse Cheyenne to us several years ago. And now apparently she released Cinnamon, however he was unable to graze due to his advancing age and defective teeth. Once again, another horse came to us with frightened eyes, barely able to walk from near starvation. How long had he been wandering about before he came to us? This tall, long-legged roan gelding? Perhaps she thought he would be fine. He was not. Initially, I began feeding him Senior Equine (a food source created for elderly horses) every morning with Snowy and afterwards Cinnamon would leave and make the slow six mile round trip to his home to see if she was there. She was not, and he returned with sad eyes to another meal. It became increasingly more difficult for him to make this journey daily as the heat was so intense and he could not maintain his weight. Soon he could no longer walk the long distance, he decided to stay and ate the much needed equine four times a day. Slowly he gained weight but it required many months for the sadness in his eyes to leave. We renamed him Cimarron and he remains with us to this day, healthy and happy. He is 36 years old and I love him dearly.

Several weeks have passed and still no word from the grant writer and no check in the mail. And so we waited and as the days grew shorter the heat became more intense as did the flies of which I'd not experienced since coming to my beloved Land of Enchantment. My body was struggling to do even the smallest of tasks, as I sweated even while painting. I had a physical examination at the Cerrillos Clinic and my blood pressure had gone up even higher. My doctor insisted I increase the dosage of the diuretic I had grudgingly been taking for two years. But she had been my doctor for ten years and she knew my lifestyle. How could she be wrong?

Several days later I began to rest in the afternoons, something I'd never done my entire life. I became irritated, agitated and lethargic... not sleeping well. I thought it was the heat. I was wrong. Bobbie our friend and retired nurse, decided to pay me a visit. "You don't look well, Karin," she said, while taking my blood pressure. It was Saturday afternoon, and I decided to call the clinic for an appointment on Monday.

Bobbie left the blood pressure monitor with me and called the next morning to see how I was feeling. She had a gut feeling something was wrong. I did not feed the animals that morning and stayed in bed feeling so dizzy and determined to go to the clinic the following day, but this would not happen. Bobbie called later in the day and became worried. She called a doctor friend of hers and told her of my symptoms. It was around six o'clock in the evening and I was now feeling nauseated and Bobbie called again. Her friend informed her that my blood pressure was not high enough to cause the dizziness...it must be dehydration. She told me to drink as much water as I possibly could and I would begin to feel better. "But if you don't feel better girl-friend," she said, "you call me and we'll go to the ER."

The more water I drank the more nauseated I became, and after several hours and taking my blood pressure again, I called Bobbie. "It was 189 over 101, Bobbie. Andy's phone must be turned off. Can you come and get me?" "Pack a bag, Karin, I'll be there in 20," she said in her army nurse voice.

Another angel was coming. Twenty minutes later she called me at our gate. "The gate is locked, Karin. You'll have to go over and wake up Andy." I have no idea where the strength came from but I found a cane and a flashlight and opened my door to walk to his house. To my utter astonishment every one of the horses were outside my door. Somehow they knew I was in trouble and were surrounding me with their love. Staggering through them I made my way to Andy's house... the little mare Lily never leaving my side. A startled Andy jumped in his truck and went down to open the gate.

The ride to the hospital was a blur. The woman at the ER who checked my vital signs did not believe anything was wrong. I was told to wait my turn. But an angel doctor looked at me and immediately put me in a room where blood was drawn. Ten minutes later, I was attached to all sorts of monitors and a saline solution was dripping into my body. Bobbie informed me I was dehydrated and my sodium level dangerously low with the electrolytes off the chart, and that "we made it just in time, girlfriend." Andy and Bobbie left me in the ER alone to make the long drive home and within a few hours I began to feel better. I began to feel grateful. Sleep did not come to me that night.

The next morning I was in a room, watching TV and eating the best grilled cheese sandwich ever created, when Andy and Bobbie returned. Bobbie said, "that was a close call, girlfriend. Glad you called me." The nurses rotated shifts every four hours and every four hours they would ask me the same question. "How did this happen?" I would tell them my story as they looked at me in disbelief. The next day as some of my friends were planning to visit me, my attending doctor, (whom I'd never seen), arrived to examine me before signing the release forms. When they took the IV out and I stood up the dizziness and nausea began. "Don't worry she said the lightheadedness will be gone in a week. Rest for the first week and then begin to do a little more everyday. You will be fine." I went home to the little house, to my dogs Gracie and Rocky with their wagging dog tails, surrounded by the mountains and manure, horses and cows... to rest.

But the symptoms of the dizziness and nausea returned and the following Sunday I was back at the ER...only this time frightened for my life. They put me in a room immediately and hooked my body up to their monitors, took a blood sample and stuck an IV in my wrist and did an EKG. I hate to admit this, but I was afraid of dying...there was so much more to do. A doctor appeared. "There is absolutely nothing wrong with you," she said. "We will keep you here until the IV runs out." They did and I returned home. Bobbie did not quite believe the doctor in the ER and called her doctor friend, the one she called a week earlier, and made an appointment for me two days later.

She was like an angel to me, the kindest, most sincere doctor I'd ever met. Young and pretty, with long black hair and big brown eyes... Dr. Como was her name. The nausea and dizziness began to leave the moment I met her. She was a true healer. Her first question was, "what medication have you been taking?" When I mentioned the name of the diuretic, she knew the answer which baffled the nurses at the hospital. Some people react to this drug and you are one of them. The nausea would leave but I had to begin eating simple foods such as rice and bananas and slowly regain my normal diet because my stomach was quite irritated from the ordeal. She told me to drink a glass of red wine every night to help me sleep. Is she a real doctor I thought? "Your condition was very rare...they did not know how to treat you at the hospital. It will take your body as long as you have been taking that diuretic to completely recover, but you will be back to as normal as possible when the temperature drops below freezing, maybe December." We left for home and I began to slowly regain my health.

What have I done? Was this a wake-up call to slow down? Why did this happen to me? Another test, I suppose. Perhaps it was a balance which was needed? I have no answers.

Chapter Seventeen

A wave of energy is about to descend and envelope your Earth.
It comes closer and closer...a time the stars and the heavens
have awaited... history in the making. You are here to witness
and work through this time of transition.
And as your beloved Gabriel promised,
"you have to do it first."

CERRILLOS, NEW MEXICO – SEPTEMBER 2012
OLD WINDMILL TRAIL

I have been home recuperating, surrounded by Rocky and Gracie and the many animals of fur, hooves and feathers. Andy took full responsibility of the daily chores for a few weeks. Slowly I began to heal and feed Snowy and Cimarron three times a day. It was not easy, but it was necessary. Bobbie sent canvases to me with encouragement and hints to begin painting once again. I looked at them for a few weeks...too depressed to even pick up a brush.

While living through this recuperation, I seemed to have put the grant out of my mind, until we were informed the grant money began to be disbursed in August and it might take a few months until it arrived. This did not feel right. Something was amiss. Sound familiar?

During this period, my dog Gracie was not herself, not as perky as usual. She began urinating on the floors and needed to see a vet. Andy took her as he was afraid I was not well enough to do it, and he was probably right. When he returned with her from the veterinarian, he told me she was diabetic. My beautiful Gracie. She needed a shot of insulin twice a day, and special food...much care and observation was required. And so began the daily shots of insulin. She seemed better for a while at least.

CERRILLOS, NEW MEXICO – OCTOBER 2012
OLD WINDMILL TRAIL

The skies in Autumn are indescribable in New Mexico. It is dusk and while sitting in my sunroom, the full moon becomes visible as it peeks above the blue-grey clouds as the sun sets behind the Sacred Hill. The skies turn pink and orange and I ask, "how much better can it get?" How much more can I feel? How much more can I do? My recuperation has lasted longer than anticipated. The dehydration must have been ongoing for many months, they told me. You must rest more, they told me. And yet the impatience grows within to get past this and move forward. The moon shows itself again over the rocky cliffs and winks at me and I hear, "within the stillness much growth is attained. Be patient." As the sky becomes dark, I go to my bed... to my dreams.

SANTA FE, NEW MEXICO – OCTOBER 2012

I began painting again, to work a few days at the gallery, to drive my jeep. One morning I drove to Gracie's veterinarian's office to pick up a prescription. The little bells attached to the door went tingle, tingle, tingle as we opened it and walked inside. I moved to the counter but no one seemed to notice me. The two women behind the counter did not look up. There was a man standing next to me with a nervous looking yellow Labrador. The dog looked at us, but not the man. The clock went tick, tick, tick...and no one said a word. I said to the man, "my dog acts like yours when she comes here too. She is so nervous." He looked stunned, and a woman behind the counter said,"can I help you?"

Five days later I drove to Santa Fe, stopped at a grocery store and was standing at the deli counter. How long is she going to take? She has waited on two men who came in after me, and was about to ask another woman when I said, "I was here first." "Oh, I'm so sorry. I didn't see you."

As I walked out the door towards my Jeep, thoughts came to me about the woman at the deli counter and the incident at the veterinarians office. They did not see me, until I spoke...not at the vet's or at the deli counter. My body, at least momentarily, was in a higher dimension, and was invisible to those of this dimension. How cool was this?

CERRILLOS, NEW MEXICO – NOVEMBER 2012
OLD WINDMILL TRAIL

Gracie has been following me around wherever I go. Something is definitely wrong. The thought came to me...she is losing her eyesight, and I called her vet for an appointment. It was confirmed. "She can only see shadows, Karin. The cataracts are covering her eyes, and she requires surgery to regain her sight. We can refer you to a canine ophthalmologist and you can make an appointment. The cost will be around $3000.00." We have a grant coming in any day now, I would call her when it arrived. But it was not to be.

A week later I took Gracie back to her vet and was informed that glaucoma had settled in one eye, and would most definitely form on her other eye as well. "There is nothing we can do. We will have to remove the eyes," she said. But I said absolutely not. "There is something else we can try. You must know that your dog is feeling much pain, but I can do a procedure that will alleviate the pressure in the eyes. It may work. It may not. Under anesthesia, I will inject one eye ten times. She will not feel a thing." A week later it was done. My Gracie is fearless and a fighter and she made it through the procedure with much more ease than myself.

Dogs are incredible. And with that, began the process of adapting to her blindness. My stress level was very high to say the least, and I did my best to hide it from Gracie. Rocky had little patience with her and growled every time she walked into him. But if this was a test for Gracie, she passed with flying colors, and did not need to have the procedure repeated on her other eye. The vet has no explanation as to why, but I do.

CERRILLOS, NEW MEXICO – THANKSGIVING 2012
OLD WINDMILL TRAIL

Several weeks before the great event, I began the process of cleaning, which had largely been ignored. Both of my children were coming to Thanksgiving! Ryan's new girlfriend, Callie, would arrive later. And the preparations began. My friends Eileen, whose husband passed away recently, and Bobbie would have dinner with us, too.

Ryan and Somer flew into the Sunport in Albuquerque on Sunday and after spending a few days in Santa Fe with friends, picked up

Callie and drove to my house in the desert. The first words out of Somer's mouth were, "I'm home. Oh, Mom, it's so good to be home," and gave me a hug. She looked so beautiful. I had not seen her for two years, as the year before her vacation time was spent with her father in Kansas. Ryan picked me up off the floor with his hug and introduced me to Callie, a very pretty redhead with the most amazing green eyes. I liked her immediately...she with the gentle voice and with eyes that loved my son. I could see that Ryan and Somer released the pain of the previous year...the passing of their father.

We played games and watched movies, and we ate and we laughed. And for once, Ryan and Somer actually enjoyed spending some time with the animals...especially the horses, who showed off a bit for them... enjoying the attention. Callie, who had never been near a horse, delighted with their antics. She and Ryan hiked to the tops of the mesas, over tall cliffs, taking pictures with their phones and my heart soared to see my children so happy.

The night before Thanksgiving, Somer and I played Animal Medicine Cards. She chose several cards and I read to her what each one meant. When it was my turn, and to my astonishment, I drew the mountain lion.

It was a perfect opportunity to discuss our past lifetime together. And for the first time I told her of the life we shared together in which she played the role of my daughter, and me, her mother. We were members of the Anasazi people who lived within this part of the country hundreds of years ago. (You may remember this incident was brought to my attention by Bryan, my dowser friend, and by a psychic in El Dorado.) I told her of being attacked by a mountain lion, and my father, her grandfather in that lifetime, the medicine man of the tribe, brought me to the Sacred Hill for healing. But it was not to be, and I passed over, leaving a very young daughter (Somer) and my husband behind. My friend Karen, whom Somer knew from Ohio as a child, was my sister during that lifetime. She raised Somer after my death. "Do you know Somer, that this lifetime you are doing a balancing act with Karma? You balanced the last lifetime, by leaving me early this lifetime. I will not honor another Karmic debt, because it will simply be repeated over and over again. Let's just agree to end this now, and forgive ourselves and each other." She did. And we talked and played the cards until retiring to bed.

The morning of Thanksgiving came early to me, as did the cooking. I cooked and cooked, until Somer took over. The heat from the stove caused the dizziness to re-appear, and I relinquished the end of the meal to my daughter. "Next year, Mom, I will do the cooking."

Eight attended my dinner which ended so quickly, as they usually do. Ryan, tall, clever, and charming as ever, shed his Indigo light upon all, and Somer entertained us all with talk of her experiences in Denver. Andy spoke of his work with the troops. And then it was over. Too soon. Ryan and Callie began the enormous task of washing the dishes. Gracie, whom I was so concerned about with so many people to run into, simply slept the entire time. Bobbie left early. Somer went to bed with a migraine. It was a typical Thanksgiving.

The next day, Ryan and Callie took Somer to the airport and spent a few days in Albuquerque, and returned to my house on Sunday. They left the following day, but Ryan promised to return on Christmas.

CERRILLOS, NEW MEXICO – DECEMBER 2012
OLD WINDMILL TRAIL

As the days grow short, breathe in my love and expand to all. Everything comes to you for a reason...every blade of grass, every tree or plant, every form, every event.

My doctor was correct. My body regained its strength as the temperatures dipped below freezing. Another decision faced me. The Treasure Box Gallery was closing its doors in the final days of December. I had to find a new gallery soon. But Christmas was approaching and there was much to do. Also, Andy and I were quite concerned about our grant, so a friend who knew the "ins and outs" of large corporations decided to do some checking on her own. We would have the answer soon.

The weeks passed by quickly and the long-awaited day of the Winter Solstice, December 21st, arrived. I truly believed it to be a powerful day, although not that which the Mayans predicted so many years ago. Rather than an ending, at least to me, it marked a new beginning or rise in consciousness for Earth and all of her inhabitants. I spent several hours in prayer and meditation, yet nothing seemed to "change" until the next day. I awoke with great energy and worked for hours and hours painting. The paintings came quite easily and quickly to me, and the realization came that something indeed had occurred.

Christmas morning arrived and I love spending it with the animals, giving them special treats along with their hay. I went into the round pen to give carrots to the cows, their absolute favorite, and for some reason paid special attention to Stephanie, talking to her as I walked about. (I had no idea why I was doing this but was about to discover the reason momentarily.) I walked towards her to hand her a carrot, and while turning around to hand one to another cow, felt something pressing against my leg. And wham! My body was thrown up in the air, landing flat on my back. Standing as quickly as possible I turned to see Stephanie glaring at me. Apparently she wanted more carrots and I did not notice. When? When will this drama end? And I walked away vowing to never feed them carrots again, more embarrassed than hurt. And what am I to learn from this? But it was Christmas and Ryan was coming and soon I forgot about the incident. (I did feed them carrots again, although with a watchful eye on Stephanie.)

Ryan drove over from Kansas City to visit us, and spent Christmas Eve in Santa Fe enjoying the farolito walk at dusk, arriving on Christmas Day to cook his famous lasagna. I assisted. The gentle giant, my son, took over the kitchen, and oh so very quickly and efficiently cooked the best lasagna I have ever tasted. My friend, Eileen, and Andy came for dinner...a quiet dinner compared to Thanksgiving. Eileen brought a beautiful salad and tasty dessert. After dinner, Ryan and I made phone calls and watched movies.

The next day, after feeding the animals, Andy gave me the bad news. His friend received the answer from the large corporation. Had our grant been approved we would have been contacted and received the funding over a month ago. She was told that in fact the grant did not fit their guidelines and was submitted too late to be even considered. How could we have believed this? How had we been fooled so completely? Andy contacted the grant writer who continued with her story, but it was one in which we no longer believed.

I had to put all of this aside because Ryan was leaving after breakfast. As I watched him drive away, the tears began to fall down my face for I knew it would be such a long time until I saw him...the anger took over. I was angry at myself for believing everything I was told about the grant. I was angry at myself for giving my power away. I was angry. Not at all a good place to be...for everything happens in Divine Order.

A few days before the New Year I walked the familiar streets of Madrid in search of a new gallery and was accepted in two of them. A well-known, established gallery took my paintings on rocks and tripled the prices. Another gallery took my paintings and prints and cards. Life was good once again, a very important decision made, and I looked forward to the New Year. The anger was forgotten and another beginning began. How much better can it get?

Chapter Eighteen

Blessed are you My Children, who walk the path of freedom within my domain of love and light. How courageous have you all been within the restrictions of duality. Now is the time to be that which you truly are. It is time to become.

CERRILLOS, NEW MEXICO – JANUARY 2013
OLD WINDMILL TRAIL

The sun chose to light the dark, expansive winter skies this day, tinting the mountains with a pinkish hue in my part of the world. January has arrived, and the old timers have predicted an early spring. It does not seem possible as I walk down to the pond to break and clear the ice in the stock tanks, my feet crunching in the snow. Yet I await the song of the western meadowlark as I have done for the past twelve years. And as the chopping begins, chop, chop, chop...until... the melodious sound is heard and the familiar feathers of gold and black are in plain sight. Yes. The old-timers are correct.

CERRILLOS, NEW MEXICO – MARCH 20, 2013
OLD WINDMILL TRAIL

The March winds blow with great force with its message...listen, listen, listen. The dust scatters and flies, twirling round and round, forming dust devils who take on an energy all to themselves...their lives short-lived. Change...the winds whisper...change. As the skies turn a murky brown, and the coyotes sing, and the horses whinny, my thoughts turn to the ending of my book. It has been a year.

It is with great sadness and relief that I write the familiar words "Old Windmill Trail" for the last time. I have made my deadline, accomplished my goal, released my life until this point. In a few months my body will become sixty years of age, though my soul is much older. What have I learned? I have learned the dance of life within a universe filled with contrasting energy, surrounded by love and light. It has been suggested that my life has been tragic, yet I think not. Look at all I've accomplished... what wisdom I've gained. And if you have come this far with me on my journey, perhaps you have come to respect, appreciate, and love those within the forms of fur and hooves and feathers as I do. They came here to assist us you know... the ones like you and me...the ones with two legs. They are as we are...

simply in a different form. How much better can it get?

What will the new Earth look like? And the remembrance of Metatron's words come to me. "You simply will awaken one day and walk outside and everything will seem 'different,' brighter, and you will feel lighter and brighter. You may not even be aware of it."

Perhaps it will be as simple as that.

Peace be with you, love and abundance.

Karin Brandi

My life continues and there will be a sequel as another new beginning has already formed. This book was written within a particular step on my ladder of spiritual growth. Please forgive my ego...it was written as it was felt through my heart at that particular moment.

About The Author

I was born in Zanesville, Ohio in 1953 and lived there until I went to college and attained a bachelor's degree in Art Education at Ohio University in 1975. I was not only the first grandchild on either side of my family to attend college, but to graduate. My parents were Roy and Juanita Williams.

At the age of five I decided to become an artist, due to the encouragement of my kindergarten teacher and my mother, and have continued on that path to this day. In my late twenties, I became the Assistant Art Director at Roach, Inc. in Columbus, Ohio. In my late thirties, I became the Art Director of an embroidery company known as 5B's and located in Zanesville, Ohio. I gave birth to my two children during this time and experienced living in Rochester, Houston, Indianapolis, and Clearwater, before moving to New Mexico.

Upon arriving to New Mexico in 1996, my life began again. I gave up my graphic design career and decided to focus on becoming a creative artist. I studied spirituality, or whatever you choose to call it, with a teacher in Albuquerque and with another teacher in Cochiti Lake for many years. In 2002, my partner and I, after moving to a remote area which is off the grid, formed a non-profit animal sanctuary known as the Olde Windmill Trail Farm Animal Sanctuary. I became the director, and the writing of my book began because of my love for the animals.

So you see, I really have no credentials to speak of for writing this book, except my life experience ... but what a life I have experienced.

Acknowledgments

*I wish to dedicate this book to all of you who read it,
as it was written for you.*

*To our Creator for giving me the gift of life,
the free will to express myself through writing,
and for constant encouragement and love.
Together, we wrote this book.*

*To my mother for her great wisdom,
and to my son Ryan and my daughter Somer
for entering into my life and teaching me unconditional love.*

*And a very special thank you to my
publisher and editor Barbara.*

CPSIA information can be obtained
at www.ICGtesting.com
Printed in the USA
FFOW04n2149091217
43994408-43162FF

9 780692 962817